I0111555

The Ragged Thirteen
Territory Bushrangers

DEREK PUGH OAM

With a foreword by
His Honour Professor the Honourable Hugh Heggie AO PSM,
23rd Administrator of the Northern Territory

Text © Dr Derek Pugh OAM (h.c.) 2024
Images: Photographs ©Derek Pugh except as referenced in captions.

All rights reserved. No part of this publication may be reproduced, stored in a retrieval system, or transmitted in any form by any means, electronic, mechanical, photocopying recording or otherwise, without the prior written permission of the author.

Pugh, Dr. Derek: Author
Title: The Ragged Thirteen: Territory Bushrangers

Design and layout by Mikaela Pugh: mikaelaapughh@gmail.com

Printed (paperback) ISBN: 9780645737479
eBook ISBN: 9780645737486

Notes: Includes bibliographical references and index.

Subjects:
Northern Territory History
East Kimberley
The Ragged Thirteen
Bushrangers
Drovers
Cattle stations of the N.T. and W.A.
Halls Creek gold rush
Aboriginal Australians

NATIONAL LIBRARY OF AUSTRALIA

A catalogue record for this book is available from the National Library of Australia

Acknowledgements

His Honour Professor the Honourable Hugh Heggie AO PSM, 23rd Administrator of the Northern Territory, has provided a foreword that is complimentary, inciteful and articulate, and I thank him sincerely for his time and effort in reading the draft text and his considered response.

Thanks also go to many others, without whom this book may not have seen the light of day. Chief among them are my travelling companions, Harry and Roy Pugh in the desert, and Sue and Graham Hiley AM and Alister Lindsay in our exploration of the Ragged Thirteen's trail to Halls Creek. Sue Hiley showed extraordinary stoicism when dragged through swamps and mountain walks while suffering from a fractured toe.

For their hospitality, thanks go to Julie Richter and her staff at Victoria River Downs Station, Lynne Leigh at Ambalindum (Hale River). For his local knowledge, I thank Ranger Tom Leather at Arltunga, and for her generous sharing of her recording of the late Billy Fitz, thanks go to Kylie Stevenson.

Readers and editors are an essential part of the preparation of any texts, and for this I particularly thank Peter Whelan AM, Graham Hiley AM, Ted McFadyen, and Mikaela Pugh.

Indigenous Australians are advised that, as this is a history, it necessarily contains the names and images of people who are now deceased.

The publication of this book has been assisted by the Northern Territory Government through the History Grants Program.

Contents

Maps

Foreword

His Honour Professor the Honourable Hugh Heggie AO PSM
Administrator of The Northern Territory

It is always with great anticipation that we await the latest publication of Dr Derek Pugh, one of the Northern Territory's foremost historians. He has written many fascinating accounts of Northern Territory settlement history and proves he is a careful researcher, deeply engaged in history and he can spin a fine yarn indeed!

As an educator in the Northern Territory, working in many locations, from large urban senior schools to remote homeland centre schools in Central Arnhem Land, as well as in international schools around the globe, it is clear that Dr Pugh brings a passion for knowledge and that you will learn a great deal through each of his works.

It is so important to write about history and Dr Pugh has done a great service in recording Northern Territory's rich tapestry of history and culture. He is preserving memory – the memories and experiences of communities and individuals – and making sure they are not forgotten. And to delve into our history is to learn more about ourselves, the roots of our communities and society plus the past actions that have shaped our present.

Who knew that the Northern Territory had its own bushrangers? While their story has faded in the present, the past has many outback tales of them to tell. It sounds like the Ragged Thirteen came together for company and safety, to survive amidst poverty and possibly to have a very good time. I invite you to read on and decide whether they were loveable larrikins or rascally criminals.

Of course, this is not just a book about a group of 13 men. It is a tale of the land where they lived and roamed plus all the people who lived there: pastoralists, travellers, miners, cattlemen, duffers, diggers and tribal Aboriginal people, from the Territory, Britain, China, Singapore, other parts of Europe and other parts of Australia.

What a rich and complex history we can celebrate as Territorians. My hearty congratulations to Dr Pugh on his magnificent contributions to Territory history, especially in uncovering and telling the stories that no one else has. Now, I invite you, dear reader, to dive into the story of the Ragged Thirteen. You are in for a treat.

Preface

Late in the nineteenth century there were plenty of cattlemen, travellers, and prospectors travelling through the dust of the Northern Territory and the Kimberley. Their weary feet trod the trails that ran between the telegraph stations and out to newly settled cattle stations. Mostly white men, they were isolated from the police or any form of authority, and some felt so unimpeded by the laws of the day, they were happy to duff cattle and steal a horse or two along the way – who was to stop them? Many met up with fellow overlanders in the wayside pubs or billabong camps along the way and joined them for companionship or safety. Thirteen of them, on the road and hungry for the gold being discovered in Western Australia, joined together in the rush to Halls Creek in 1886. They were expert bushmen who valued horses and other men's cattle highly, but with little funds and dressed in rags, they were also happy to take what they needed. Their crimes formed them into a gang, arguably the only gang of bushrangers the Top End was ever to see. This book tells the story of these 'ragged thirteen'.

The 1880s were a tough time in the bush of the Northern Territory and the Kimberley of Western Australia. Pastoralists, travellers, and miners were in a constant battle with both the elements and the local Indigenous tribes. It was a frontier of death and violence, with few constraints on the behaviour of the white invaders. In 1886, hundreds of hopeful gold miners rushed through this frontier, heading for the gold at Halls Creek. Some were on foot, pushing wheelbarrows, but others, with either the funds to buy horses or the nerves to steal them, rode on what became well-trodden tracks through the bush.

The majority of the population of the Northern Territory of South Australia and the Kimberley were tribal people. Their ancestors had prospered for thousands of years in a wide range of environments, from the harsh deserts of the interior to the tropical coasts and escarpment country of the north. They had no concept of the changes that would be brought to them by the newcomers.

British men and women arrived during the first half of the nineteenth century to settle at one of three settlements they attempted to establish on the coast, but these had come and gone. A South Australian attempt, at the mouth of the Adelaide River, had similarly collapsed in 1866.

But then, in February 1870, a new batch of South Australian settlers arrived to carve out their new homes in Palmerston, on the shores of Port Darwin. They were mostly from Adelaide, keen on a new life in South Australia's northern colony. By 1886, their numbers were still small. According to the best figures we have, 966 Europeans then lived in the Territory[1]. Sixty of them were miners in the bush, and most of the rest lived in Palmerston. But they weren't alone. Other newcomers in the Territory had come from China and Singapore. In the same year, there were 3,237 Chinese men and women resident in Palmerston or Southport[2], and a thousand or more in the goldfields, or working on the railway. A few Chinese men were also employed by white men in the bush, usually as cooks.

Apart from the mines, the Europeans could be found on cattle stations, in the telegraph repeater stations spread along the Overland Telegraph Line or travelling along on the dirt tracks between these isolated outposts. Gatherings of Europeans, mostly men, but also a growing number of women, could also be found in numerous wayside pubs, in the tiny service and supply towns of Borroloola and Katherine, and in the mining camps of Burrundie, Pine Creek, and later, in Arltunga and Stuart (Alice Springs). There were not many of them. A few of the newcomers undoubtedly remain anonymous, but most had their names recorded in the census and/or were mentioned in the newspapers by local correspondents.

Then, in 1886, more travellers arrived. There was gold at Halls Creek in the Kimberley, and thousands joined the rush, and headed there to seek their fortunes. Travelling men would join up with their fellows for company and safety to cross the Territory.

They often soon returned, broken, as the diggings failed.

A group of thirteen of these men met and stayed together at a time when numbers gave them strength to do anything and get away with it. They were 'on the never never', in the remote back blocks of the Northern Territory and the Kimberley, for just a few months in 1886, but they became famous for their exploits. They came from South Australia, Queensland, New South Wales, New Zealand, and Scotland, and they shared a lust for adventure and looked forward to the gold that awaited them in the Kimberley.

Every one of them was a talented horseman, with bush survival skills they could rely on, but unfortunately they had very little money. To survive, and have fun, they ran riot on the overlanders' trail, duffing cattle at will and holding up wayside pubs and cattle stations with impunity. Together they drove a small herd of stolen horses west to the Halls Creek goldfields.

They came to be called the *Ragged Thirteen*, and they became the Territory's only bushranger gang – or at least, they came the closest to being a gang of bushrangers that we ever had.

Today they are almost forgotten. They got away with their crimes. Not one was arrested or ever faced a court of law. Instead, some became highly respected community members and family men.

This book also tells stories of some of the growing number of pioneer pastoralists, drovers, miners, and explorers, and their often-disastrous interactions with the local Aboriginal people, across the Top End. Contemporaries of the men of the Ragged Thirteen, their stories give context for the behaviour of the gang and set the scene for all overlanders of that era.

As the Ragged Thirteen coped with their poverty by living off the land, duffing cattle, passing dud cheques, raiding shanty pubs, bush stores, and cattle stations, they had a fine time. With few scruples about helping themselves, and basking in the largesse of the powerful, they were happy to share their booty, Robin Hood-like, with fellow travellers.

For a few decades, the Thirteen were famous. Known as the 'Ragged Thirteen' everywhere, it was, nevertheless, a part of their success to remain as anonymous as possible. They used nicknames and, when they were no longer thirteen, but one or two, they were mostly unrecognisable. For fifty or more years, stories about them were legion, and dozens of 'wannabes' boasted that they were a part of the notorious gang. Nevertheless, tales of the exploits of the real gang entertained travellers around campfires for decades, and theirs is a story that should continue to be told.

Sorting out the wheat from the chaff is one aim of this book.

Northern Australia, for all its rogues and rascals, has little claim to having had any 'bushrangers' in the nineteenth century. Were the Ragged Thirteen real bushrangers? There are arguments for and against. The Northern Territory papers of the day, *The North Australian and The Northern Territory Times and Gazette*, were silent about them, despite eagerly repeating tales of the famous, but more murderous, bushrangers from the southern colonies. Their short existence as a gang perhaps meant that they came and went before the news of their exploits arrived in Palmerston. They never 'bailed up' a stagecoach like highwaymen, nor killed anyone, as far as we know. Nor were they 'career criminals.' When the gang broke up, each drifted off to other occupations, and mostly went straight and became respectable.

As a result, little is known about them, and almost all of it comes from later memoirs or journalists seeking out the story. Ernestine Hill, for example, interviewed men in the 1930s who knew some of the Thirteen, and in 1951 called them "laughing cavaliers" and "light-hearted scamps riding together, gentle grafters of the Great

Unknown, soldiers of outback fortune and, in a hungry country, out for all they could get".[3]

Pioneer cattleman John Durack recalled in 1959 that they were "very amateur bushrangers" who "never succeeded in terrorising the countryside as they dreamed of doing".[4]

Miner and cattlemen, Thomas Traine, in his *Memories and Experiences as a Pioneer*, wrote in 1912, that the Ragged Thirteen's leader, Tom Holmes (Nugent), had told him that it was all a joke, and once the name was awarded, the group of thirteen played up to it, and that created the legend[5]. Traine claimed that a man named Cashman had carried the joke forward and warned everyone that the "Ragged Thirteen are coming," and soon everyone was worried about a mythical gang of tattered desperados.

Fiction authors cope with the paucity of information by neatly merging what is known with rollicking outback tales of their travels across the Territory, to the Halls Creek goldfields, adding to their stories all the other characters of note who made the papers in those days. Many of these people were named Jack. There was Russian Jack, Red Jack, and Māori Jack Reid, to name three[6]. To these authors, the Ragged Thirteen were 'larrikins' on the run.

To the State Library of South Australia, they were 'Tea and Sugar Bushrangers,' a term which the gang might have found insulting, but others saw them either as 'the scum of four colonies, fugitives from justice'[7], or 'brilliant horsemen, fugitives, consummate bushmen, lovers of bush poetry and champions of the underdog'[8].

Could they have been all these things?

The Ragged Thirteen were a small part of the thousands of men, and a few women, who joined the Halls Creek goldrush. So, is this a rags-to-riches story about gold? No. As far as we know, they found very little, but the time they spent travelling to the goldfields is much more memorable, and what happened to each of them afterwards, even more fascinating.

The Ragged Thirteen were a product of their time. To understand them, we need to know the people who lived and died around them: the station managers, cattlemen and drovers, miners, storekeepers, sly-grog shanty owners, Overland Telegraph Line workers, and travellers. These people were colonial Australians, English, Scottish, New Zealanders, Chinese, 'Afghans'[9], Malays, 'Manila men', Norwegians, Russians, and others, all of them doing their best to survive in the most remote part of the British Empire.

And, of course, there were many Indigenous people, whose ancestors had lived and died in their traditional lands for millennia before them. Tribal Aboriginal people lived their lives bound to their country and the predictability of the ecosystems they were a part of. They had no concept of the British Empire, but they knew the boundaries that separated them from their neighbours, and they defended them according to ancient laws and customs. The newcomers, particularly the pastoralists, knew and cared little about tribal boundaries, traditionally owned country, or the ecosystem the locals relied upon. They took the country as vacant land, and their cattle trampled the vegetation, muddied the waterholes, and broke the food chains that local people were a part of. As bush food became harder to find, and sheep and cattle easier, conflict with the settlers was inevitable.

This conflict was old news in the inland plains of Queensland, where the 'Native Police' had been clearing the land of Aboriginal families for decades[10]. But it was mostly still to come in the Northern Territory of the 1880s, as herds of cattle and flocks of sheep arrived, and overlanders, pastoralists and policemen alike were armed to the teeth with the latest Snider carbines.

The story starts, therefore, with some of the bushmen who brought in the first herds and flocks, and those who stayed to develop the land they claimed as their own.

Endnotes

1 Jones, 1987.
2 Jones, 1987.
3 Hill, 1951.
4 Durack, 1959.
5 Traine, 2005.
6 *The Ragged Thirteen: Stories of Australia's Northern Frontier in the 1880s*, by Judy Robinson (2002), and Greg Barron's novel *Red Jack and the Ragged Thirteen* (2019).
7 *Toowoomba Chronicle and Darling Downs Gazette*, 18 October 1924, page 13.
8 Greg Barron, *The Ragged Thirteen: "Tea and Sugar" Bushrangers*, https://go55s.com.au/lifestyle.
9 To the 19th century white Australian population, an 'Afghan' was anyone who came from countries that traditionally used camels, including Afghanistan, Egypt, Pakistan, and others.
10 Marr, 2023.

Chapter 1
Drovers, Sheep, and Cattle

In the early days of settlement in North Australia, golden pastures beckoned cattlemen and shepherds to the Northern Territory[1] and the Kimberley, like the golden nuggets that called miners in later years. Cattle were driven overland on stock routes that became well-trodden through Western Queensland, and sheep were brought north in their thousands along the Overland Telegraph Line (OTL).

Ralph Milner was the first in with sheep. He brought 2,000 from South Australia to feed the work crews constructing the OTL in 1870[2]. These were quickly consumed, and more were needed to established breeding populations. Several stations tried to run sheep, and the Western Kimberley was originally settled by sheep farmers, but cattle proved to be more economically viable, and it remains so today.

Horses and cattle were first brought overland in 1872. Driven from Burketown in Queensland, the drovers were Dillan Cox and Wentworth D'Arcy Uhr. They followed Ludwig Leichhardt's 1845 route via the Limmen-Bight, McArthur River, and Roper River, and crossed the lands of the Garrwa, Yanyuwa, Binbinka, and Alawa peoples, with about four hundred head of cattle. On at least four occasions they needed to fight their way through with their Westley Richards carbines and revolvers. D'Arcy Uhr also had a military Martini-Henry rifle, accurate over hundreds of metres, and with a background as a policeman leading a squad of the notorious Native

Police in Queensland, he sure knew how to use it[3]. When Uhr's Martini-Henry 'made its voice heard' to a group of Binbinka warriors, wrote stockman James Barry, 'they halted in astonishment to pick up their comrade, who seemed stricken down by magic'[4]. Without any concept of the advanced technology facing them, the Binbinka fell, and kept falling, to 'writhe or lay forever motionless' among their comrades.

In this way, Uhr and his men forged their stock route through hostile country that, over the next few decades, would take more than 200,000 head of cattle from Queensland into the Territory, laying waste to the local tribes and their grasslands, rivers, and pristine streams along the way.

Cox and Uhr lost many of their horses in the bush near the Roper River. Cox's plan had been to sell his cattle to hungry miners in the rapidly growing goldfields south of Palmerston, but the horses were to be bred for the British Army in India. He applied for a pastoral lease of 115,000 acres on the Douglas Peninsula in October 1872, but was unsuccessful in his application. The land is still called Cox Peninsula, after Dillon Cox, because he nevertheless founded *Bowerlee Station*[5] there, albeit unofficially. His tenure was short, because he was soon stabbed in the kidney during a fight with his nephew and died of his wounds, after two weeks of suffering[6].

The second mob of cattle was brought to Palmerston by George de Latour, from Townsville, on 19 October 1874. They were yarded at Knuckey's Lagoon, a few kilometres south of Port Darwin, and were immediately sold for meat at more than £20 a head. None was left to breed and establish a local cattle industry.

On his overland return to Queensland, de Latour picked up a large mob of horses, which were some of those lost by Cox, and sold them in Normanton. He then returned to the Limmen-Bight region to look for more[7].

The first official cattle stations leased in the Territory were Glencoe Station[8], 145 km (90 mi) southwest of Katherine, and

Figure 1: Springvale Station on the Katherine River (Foelsche, SLSA, ph0754-0015).

Springvale Station near Katherine. The 5,900 km² Glencoe lease was first assigned in 1878 to Messrs Travers and Gibson, with Mr Burkitt as its manager[9]. The first cattle were brought to Glencoe by James Warby in 1879, following D'Arcy Uhr's overland route, and Nat Buchanan brought in more a few months later. By 1884, Glencoe Station was stocked with about 7,000 head of mixed cattle and four hundred horses, but it was by no means the largest cattle station. That was the new Victoria River Downs (VRD), at 41,155 km².

VRD spread across Bilingara and Karranga native lands, It was taken up by Charles Fisher and Maurice Lyons (who also took over Glencoe Station in 1881). The two stations were soon stocked with 20,000 head of cattle that Nat Buchanan brought in from Queensland, after the largest cattle drive in history. By 1886, VRD ran more than 25,000 head of cattle, and by 1907, almost 70,000.

Springvale Station, on the Katherine River, was first leased in June 1879. A South Australian pastoralist named Dr W.J. Browne employed two brothers, Alfred[10], and Arthur Giles, to set up and

Figure 2: Glencoe Station on Brock Creek, 1883 (Foelsche, B-10129).

Figure 3: Alfred Giles and family, Springvale Homestead, Katherine, NT, July 1893 (SLSA ph0111-0001).

manage the station. Alfred brought 12,000 sheep from the Flinders Ranges, along the Overland Telegraph Line, and Arthur brought 3,000 cattle, in mobs of 500, from the upper Darling River region. The sheep did not do well. The flock failed to survive and there was very little wool ever exported. When Dr Browne left the Territory, in 1887, he had lost nearly £50,000[11].

The Territory's land rush continued into the 1880s, when 1.3 million km² of land across the Territory were applied for as pastoral holdings. Some of them soon became well known, like Victoria River Downs, Newcastle Waters, Marrakai, Elsey[12], Brunette Downs, Corrella Downs, and Daly River Stations. Others came and went like the seasons.

Harry Redford

Figure 4: Harry Arthur Redford (FL2868206).

There was a famous novel, written in 1888, called *Robbery Under Arms*[13], by Thomas Browne. Its main character was Captain Starlight[14], a gentleman bushranger, who was a horseman of note, and a hero to the cockies of the outback. The author claimed that Starlight was a montage of outback characters he had met, or heard of, and that in the mix was a real-life bushman named Harry Arthur Redford (aka Readford).

In later years, Redford became a manager of cattle stations in the Northern Territory, and eventually a station owner, but he was known to Thomas Browne as a bold Queenslander, and the greatest cattle duffer of them all!

When Harry Redford was labelled 'Starlight', probably no one was more surprised than he. He certainly never called himself 'Captain Starlight', nor thought of himself as a bushranger, but his exploits lead into the beginning of the story of the Ragged Thirteen.

In 1869, Harry Redford was a 27-year-old squatter on a property near Windorah, in Queensland, named Wombundery. An expert bushman with extensive experience in droving cattle, he noticed, on his travels through western Queensland, that some properties were so large that their owners rarely, if ever, visited the most remote parts of their land, upon which flourished large numbers of 'cleanskin' cattle. Stations like Bowen Downs, near Barcaldine, in Central Queensland, for instance, spread across two million acres. Redford concluded that a few cattle gently removed from the station's remotest regions would never be missed.

Cattle duffing, as it was known, hardly seemed like a crime (unlike *rustling*, as the same practice was called in the Americas). Drovers always lost a few cattle and collected a few strays on every trip, and 'cleanskins' were fair game, they thought. Gathering up a cleanskin was called 'poddy-dodging', and, if some were not 'clean', and a few brands needed to be changed to ensure their new owners' ease of conscience, well, where was the harm in that? Duffing and poddy-dodging were so common in the 1800s, that most cattlemen were more or less guilty. But in 1873, Redford took the practice to a new level.

Bowen Downs station is crossed by the Thomson River, as it winds its way southwest to become the Barcoo River and Cooper Creek, and eventually finds Lake Eyre. The station was carved out of Iningai country[15], and settled in 1862 by a company of eight investors, led by William Landsborough and Nathaniel Buchanan. Nat Buchanan, of whom we'll hear more later, was the station's first manager, but he abandoned his share to drought in 1867. He may have regretted this decision, because within three years, Bowen Downs was one of the most successful runs in Australia. The station stretched 200 km across Mitchell Grass plains and supported a herd of 60,000 cattle.

It was a share of these cattle that held Redford's interest in 1873. He recruited three others (Dewdney, McKenzie, and Rooke), and they quietly built cattle yards in a hidden gully near the river. When they were ready, they mustered small herds of cattle, thirty or so at a time, and kept them yarded until they had about three hundred beasts. They then drove these to a small property, about 40 km south, and repeated the process until there were about 1,000 head, ready to go. Under Redford's leadership, the duffers then drove them south-east to South Australia, passing the Barcoo and following the Cooper Creek. They were careful. When passing settled areas for example, which was rare, they divided the mob into smaller herds so the dust clouds they created were less obvious to any casual observer.

Their tracks were visible for longer, however, and the local land baron of the Cooper area, John Costello, easily spied them and, because he knew of no drovers passing that way, he made enquiries. Mary Durack wrote that this "caused western graziers to investigate their runs"[16] and it wasn't long before a thousand head of Bowen Downs cattle were noted as missing.

Redford's plan relied on reports he heard of rainfall in the Cooper's channels, and the south-western corner of Queensland, earlier in the year. Rain meant the waterholes would be full, and there would be enough grass for the herd, he thought. He was right – the grass was knee-deep by the time they arrived at the Strzelecki Creek area, three months later. By June, they had travelled almost 1,300 km to arrive at the Artrocoona Native Well. The men were running out of supplies so, at a place called Wallelderdine, near Hawker, Redford arranged to revictual from a storekeeper named Allan Walke. It was here he made his biggest mistake.

Among the herd was a white bull that Walke took an immediate interest in, as he recognised its good breeding potential. Cattle Overseer William Butler told a packed Roma Courthouse, in 1873, that the bull was:

> … a very valuable imported bull, of pure white colour,
> branded A on the near and off rump; when he [Redford]
> selected the bull above-mentioned he placed an additional
> brand on him—namely, S on the loin…[17]

Calling himself Henry Collins, Redford had traded this distinctive animal, plus two branded cows, for clothes and stores. But Butler, who had originally purchased the bull in 1868, for the Bowen Downs Station[18], was on his trail, with his head stockman, a noted bushman named Leonard Elvey[19].

Arriving at Wallelderdin three months after Redford, Butler immediately recognised the bull as his. It was "a remarkable beast", and despite protestations from Walke that his receipts, from a 'Henry

Collins,' were genuine, he couldn't argue against the evidence of the brand.

Butler and his companions continued tracking the mob, and eventually arrived at Blanchwater Station[20], to find that the manager, J. Hawkes Mules, had not only paid Redford £5000 for the entire herd, but had already sold most of them on the Adelaide Meat Market. Nevertheless, enough evidence was gathered to ensure warrants were signed for the arrest of the duffers. Dewdney, McKenzie, and Rooke were picked up quickly, and they soon found themselves in court in Roma. Luckily for them, local sympathies ran their way, and they were declared not guilty.

It took a further 18 months for Redford to be caught. He had bought a hotel in Gulgong, N.S.W. under a different name, and was only discovered when he took a man he called 'Jew Boy' to court for stealing his cashbox.

Redford was recognised, and arrested, outside the Gulgong Court. He was then taken to Blackall to await his trial and held in 'close confinement' for a year, while the bull was collected and brought to the court as evidence. Redford 'endured hardships' there that were mentioned often by the defence lawyers at his trial.

The case was heard in the Roma Court House on 11 February 1873. The evidence produced was very convincing indeed, and Redford looked to be heading for a long gaol sentence. Judge Blakeney directed the jury towards a guilty verdict, but:

> ... the jury retired to consider their verdict at 9 o'clock and returned to Court about 10 with a verdict of 'not guilty'! The prisoner was discharged. This case lasted the whole day, from 9 a.m. to 10 p.m. The Court was crowded in every part, and much surprise was evinced at the verdict, in which the Judge joined; and, after having requested the foreman to repeat it, observed, "Thank God, gentlemen, that verdict is yours, not mine"[21].

The community was outraged. Petitions and numerous letters to politicians and newspapers decried the blatant injustice. Judge

Blakeney complained that the case could not "possibly have been better prepared by the police, or brought before the Court by the Crown, to secure a conviction"[22].

"Altogether, to my mind" wrote the judge:

… no case could possibly be clearer for a conviction than this one, and my charge to the jury was decidedly against the prisoner. Nevertheless, they returned a perverse verdict of "not guilty"[23].

The Queensland Government Executive Council was also shocked, and the official response was to cancel the criminal jurisdiction of the Roma court, for two years.

Redford was a free man by then, of course, and back droving in the Gulf Country – this time legitimately. In 1884, he took the first mob of 120 cattle to Brunette Downs Station, on the Barkly Tablelands of the Northern Territory. This 5,200 km² property, which ranged over the traditional lands of the Wambaya people, had been bought by Walter Douglas for £4,000 in 1881. Redford stayed at Brunette for several years, as the station's first manager.

Redford's name next comes up in 1883, in connection with a tragic tale of a lost police search party, from the Barrow Creek Telegraph Station. The station buildings were still under construction, and the workers lived in temporary huts, with thatched grass roofs, 'protected' by Mounted Constable John Charles Shirley.

Barrow Creek lies within the lands of the Kaytetye people, some of whom were hostile to the settlers and the station manager. Telegrapher Richard Watson was wary of them because:

…. the blacks had behaved in a threatening manner on several occasions to people who were out looking for horses; and he therefore kept them at a distance from the station and was very careful about his firearms[24].

In August that year, a message arrived saying that a teamster named J.E. Martin had been speared and killed when travelling along the telegraph lines near Lawson Springs, 45 km north of Powell Creek:

… The blacks attacked our camp at the Lawson Springs at

9

about 10.30 on the night of the 29th ult. and killed my mate
(J. E. Martin) to the best of my belief, as there was no visible
signs of life. They tried to get both of us, only I woke up in
time to save myself and my mate from being burned as well as
killed. Please send me some assistance as soon as you can. My
cook and wagons are right. J. Rees August 31.

Mr. Jones, assistant at Powell's Creek, and two men left
Powell's Creek yesterday afternoon… Arrived at wagons 11.30
last night, loading all night. Went to Springs this morning
with Rees and saw J. E. Martin; skull smashed in just above
forehead on right hand side; face covered with blood…[25]

Constable Shirley went to investigate with Telegraph
Stationmaster Alan M. Giles and six others, including two Aboriginal
trackers – Gumen and an un-named man. At the same time, Harry
Redford and some stockmen were rumoured to have also been
attacked by Aborigines at Brunette Downs Station, and they were
said to be either lost, or speared to death. Shirley's rescue party was
expected to find them as well. It seemed a likely tale, because someone
had found several of Redford's horses dead, and when Alan Giles was
asked, by telegram, of the rumours of the attack on Redford, his reply
was printed in the *Adelaide Observer*:

…yes, heard rumour of murder of Mr. Redford's party, but
think it must be some distance east of Attack Creek, as Mr.
Shirley and myself, with the police party from Tennant's
Creek, left Mr. Redford and party camped on Attack Creek,
about ten miles east of line on September 5 last…[26]

It turned out Redford was alive and well, and had made it
home, minus a few horses. Sadly, the unnecessary rescue party was
not so fortunate. They were last seen on 4 November, and all but two
of them perished of thirst about 25 km from Attack Creek. Alan Giles
survived, rescued by Gumen, an Aboriginal tracker, who came back
for him with water while he lay dying[27].

The next February, Giles returned with Mounted Constable
William Willshire to find the bodies. They recovered Shirley's bones[28],
but the rest were never seen again. Shirley had written some letters in

his last hours:

> … Travelling allowance is due to me for all the time I have been out, please pay it to my mother, also give her and my sisters and brothers my dying love; I am too weak to write anymore; I died in executing my duty. (Signed) J. C. Shirley.

On another paper addressed to 'Mr. Michael, Barrow Creek', he wrote:

> … Good-bye, old man, remember me to all on the line. J. C.[29]

In about 1885, Redford left Brunette Downs to establish Corrella Downs Station, a small property to the northwest of Brunette. He worked it until March 1901, and had several successful seasons when he took cattle to market: in 1900 for example, he drove a herd that was 'upwards of 2000 head' to Burketown for 'treatment' at the Burketown Meat Extract Works[30].

But the Gulf Region climate is fickle. At the turn of the century, it was hit by a long-lasting and devastating drought that forced Redford to pack up and leave Corrella, to seek out better land. Ironically, he then met his end by drowning in Corrella Creek whilst attempting to cross it in a flood. He was 59 years old.

Redford's efforts as a cattle duffer were legendary, but so too were his skills in droving, and several Northern Territory stations were stocked by the cattle he brought overland. His contribution to the Territory pastoral industry cannot be understated. Billy Linklater remembered him, as 'White Bull' Redford, fondly in his memoir. Writing of the 'fairness' of poddy-dodging as a community service that kept down the number of wild scrub bulls, Linklater knew that Redford would understand his philosophy:

> … I shall always remember Redford, sitting squarely on his horse, with the grave and detached dignity that characterised him, gazing into a long valley where hundreds of cattle were grazing. I could almost have sworn he smothered a sob when he said, "There they are Billy, just like plums, ripe and waiting to be picked"…[31]

Nat Buchanan

Figure 5: Nathaniel Buchanan (1900, Anon - Gooreen collection).

Nat Buchanan, as might befit a man who was most comfortable in the bush, was a man of few written words, so there are no diaries or autobiographies of his life. However, his son, Gordon Buchanan, at one time manager of Flora Valley Station, kept his father's memory alive[32] in a book he titled *Packhorse and Waterhole*, as did his grand-daughter, Roberta Buchanan, in *In the Tracks of Old Bluey*. Both are excellent sources of information about Nat.

But there are other writers who knew him as well. Charles Gaunt recalled forty years later:

> Nat Buchanan ("Old Bluey")… A grand bushman, he would, on leaving camp in the morning, fill his pockets with dried apples and be away perhaps for a couple of days. When hungry he used to eat a few apples, and this was followed by a big drink of water and Presto! In a short time, hunger was appeased and with the apples swelling up in his innards, he would be as full as a tick[33].

Another was Donald Swan, a fourteen-year-old boy with an interest in horses, who joined the drive of the very first cattle to the Kimberley. Droving had not originally been a part of Swan's life plan. He was an amateur jockey in the country races at Bogantungun, an upcountry Queensland railway terminus, on Boxing Day, 1882. A group of wild young men turned up by train from Rockhampton with horses at the races, and their leader, 22-year-old Arthur Longdon, entered some of them in a race. When they were all beaten by Swan, Longdon was impressed.

After the races he offered Swan a job, and the boy accepted immediately – he wished nothing more than to be out bush with horses and cattle and had no desire to continue as a shop-boy behind the counter at the local store. Swan had heard little of Western Australia and had no idea how long it would take to get there, but he packed up and left with the mob – without even telling his parents.

Longdon was working for Panton and Osmand, the first to take up Kimberley land near the Ord River after Alexander Forrest's exploration a few years earlier. He took 1,000 head of cattle from Beaufort Station, and another 4,000 head from Avington Station near Blackall, and drove them through Aramac and Hughenden in mobs of just over 2,000. Reaching Richmond, after an easy and well provisioned drive over excellent country, they started northwest towards the Leichhardt River. There was then a change in management. Nat Buchanan, already the most experienced drover in the Northern Territory, took over from Longdon.

Donald Swan was thrilled. "'Bluey' Buchanan is a man who should go down in history," he told the *West Australian* in 1937. "He was a great bushman, a great drover who settled many stations in the north of Australia, and a good man"[34]. Also in the crew was another consummate bushman, named Bob Button. This son of a convict was to be the manager of Ord River Station, when the cattle arrived there in June, 1884[35].

When travelling, the cattle were split into several large mobs. These travelled apart, sometimes several weeks behind each other. They were managed by parties of about ten men – a leader, teamsters, drovers, a horse-hunter, and a cook. A smaller team, sometimes just a couple of men, brought the bulls along in a separate small mob.

Buchanan, who was in charge of the whole expedition, rode backwards and forwards between the herds, managing the general progress. Each day, the cattle started off at dawn and travelled until dusk. In open country, they were allowed to spread out to graze as they moved, but near settlements they were pushed together. Each night, a watch was kept by the drovers in turn, and the last handed over to the horse-hunter before dawn, who then rounded up the horses for the drovers to use at daybreak. Donald Swan worked as a horse-hunter for most of the drove[36], and he was one of only two men who remained for its entire length. In fact, dozens of other men came and went, depending on the season and cattle movements. This made sense when, for example, the cattle were 'rested' for several months over the wet season at McArthur River, and fewer employees were needed to mind them. There were also 'packers' who travelled from Darwin, or coastal depots, to bring supplies for the teams as they were needed. It was Buchanan's success in managing these logistics that made him such a successful boss drover.

When the team nearly ran out of rations during the 3-month stay at the McArthur River, Bob Button was sent ahead to the Katherine Telegraph Station to order more provisions. It was exactly a year after Swan had been recruited at the Queensland race meeting:

> By Boxing Day, 1883, supplies were so short that there was very little sugar or flour left and everyone was put on still shorter supplies. Half-pint of flour per day per man was measured out each morning and handed to the cook to be made into as many johnny-cakes as there were men. All the measures were mixed in the one dish, but to prevent complaints and ensure a fair deal all round an ingenious method was adopted to distributing the luxury. One of the men stood with his back to the dish and as he named each man the cook gave the man named whichever johnny-cake came to hand. A few bites could finish a johnny-cake which was about the size of a biscuit[37].

Lindsay Crawford (1852-1901)

Described as a "man of splendid physique, and a fine specimen of a South Australian bushman"[38], Lindsay Crawford left school at 15, to train as a telegraph operator in 1867. However, he had a sense of adventure, and with his family's Adelaide brewing background behind him, he travelled to the new settlement of Palmerston at Port Darwin

Figure 6: Lindsay Crawford (Ex Lewis 2021).

in 1873, to start a local brewery with his father, E.J.F. Crawford[39]. When that plan didn't work, he joined the Territory's gold rush, but again found little success.

Luckily, however, telegraphy skills were much in demand, and Crawford was recruited to be an operator at Powell Creek Telegraph Station, 800 km south of Darwin. Three years later, he resigned to take over the Old Southport Store in Southport, near Port Darwin, but this was another financial loss – the difficulty in getting stock to on-sell to miners was just too great. In 1878, he returned to the employ of the Telegraph Department for the next four years, before leaving to visit his brother in New Zealand.

Five years later, in 1883, Crawford found his way back to the Territory via a novel route. He joined Ernest Favenc in a journey to explore the country, from the most western Queensland cattle properties, across the plains to the Overland Telegraph Line, and then northeast through the McArthur River region of the Gulf of Carpentaria.

Ernest Favenc and his party were the first Europeans to cross the Barkly Tablelands. There were four of them: Favenc, Crawford, and Harry Creaghe and his wife, Emily. Mrs. Creaghe was the Territory's only female explorer of the 19th Century, and her diary is an excellent record of the entire journey.

The party gathered at Gregory Downs Station in Western Queensland in early April 1883 and travelled westwards to Powell Creek Telegraph Station. It was remote and difficult country, and conditions were very tough. A lack of water and millions of flies made much of the travelling torturous. One morning, poor Crawford earned Emily's ire when she accused him of "leaving the quills in the ducks instead of plucking them clean". Creaghe had curried the ducks he had shot the evening before, for breakfast. They ate in the half-light of dawn, but when the sun came up, they saw that the quills were, in fact, thousands of flies that had found their way into the curry. The men were quite ill, she said.

Towards the end of the journey, with an 80-mile dry stage ahead of them, they had run out of water and were 'despairing' of getting any, until three miles ahead, they saw some smoke from a campfire that belonged to some Aboriginal people:

> ... We reached the fire & were going round it, when Favenc made a gallop & Crawford followed from behind... & we knew they must have seen niggers... presently we got up to them & saw Mr. Favenc holding a man with one hand & in the other pointing his revolver at him, & Crawford holding a gin. They were a peculiar sight. They had never seen white men before, we soon found out, by their showing no fear when Favenc pulled out his revolver[40].

Favenc tied the man up to stop him running away and then explained through sign language that all they wanted was to be led to water. Eventually they were taken to a small waterhole where there were "7 men & 9 gins & some piccaninnies"[41]. They were able to fill their waterbags and water the horses. They left the people unmolested but travelled four hours into the night to put distance between them – just in case.

Finally, within reach of Powell Creek, and in country Crawford and Favenc both recognised, Crawford went ahead to warn Bowley and Goss, the telegraph staff, that a woman was about to arrive. "They wouldn't believe it until they saw me" she recalled. Crawford was immediately at home and "quite in his element".

Near the station, a small group of Aboriginal people were camped. They were "not civilised" said Emily, but there was no fear of any danger:

… They are terrified at the sight of firearms, so many of them being killed at different times. The S.A. government is very strict about murdering niggers, a man is liable to be hung for it, if it is found out, so unless the blacks have killed cattle or sheep, the white men do not harm them, & then they have to keep it very quiet in case it should get to headquarters[42].

Was Crawford involved in instilling this fear during his time at the station? Later history suggests he was certainly capable of killing.

After his explorations with Favenc, Crawford found pastoral work on Richmond Downs Station that gave him valuable experience as a cattleman. The cattle barons, C.B. Fisher, and J. Maurice Lyons, then drafted Crawford to establish a new station, near the headwaters of the Victoria River, with his mate 'Greenhide' Sam Croker (who went on to manage the neighbouring Wave Hill Station[43]).

Called Victoria River Downs Station (VRD), it was to become, for a time, the largest cattle station in the world, spreading 41,133 km² across the tribal lands of an estimated 1,500 Bilingara and Karranga (aka Karangpura) people[44].

On arrival in the downs, Crawford and Croker were met with a 'shower of spears,' but they persisted, nevertheless, to establish a remote homestead and cattle yards, and prepared to accept cattle from the drovers employed to bring them from the east.

The required stores were shipped to Crawford via the Victoria River, and in May 1886 he opened a store, on the banks of the river, to be a supply depot for VRD and all other stations in the area. VRD's problem then was the need to transport the stores through Jasper Gorge to the homestead, as this was the most direct way. The route through the gorge was an incredibly difficult rocky valley, through which horses, bullock teams, and men, struggled to pass. Crawford employed a contractor named Charles Gore to improve the road through the gorge in 1885. Unfortunately, the Karangpura objected and they were continually harassed by them. Crawford provided his team with an armed guard and a pair of attack dogs, all the while hardening his attitudes towards Aboriginal people.

In 1892, W.S. Scott, the manager of Willeroo Station[45], was murdered by a group of Wardaman tribesmen:

> ... Mr. Scott was speared in the back several times, the blacks leaving the spears sticking in the body. He was also cut down the centre of the forehead, evidently with a tomahawk...[46]

Crawford went to investigate. So did Alfred Giles and Mounted Constable Browne, but they arrived at the scene a day after Crawford, on 25 October 1892:

> ... We did not see the worst of it, as Mr. Crawford – one day ahead of us – found everything taken out and broken and scattered in all directions. He collected them as well as he could, and so we found them – cases broken open and general destruction; thirty or forty fowls killed and thrown in heaps; twenty bags of flour, four or five bags of rice, and over 60lbs of tobacco, with all the pipes and matches; two dozen new Dungaree suits, two dozen pairs of boots; the whole of the Messrs Scott's wearing apparel, blankets, and rugs; four new rugs, four Winchester rifles, and 300 rounds of cartridges. All the above-mentioned articles were taken away, besides a host of other odds and ends. Had Mr. Crawford not arrived when he did, there is no doubt the total destruction of the station would have taken place. There were no niggers visible when Mr. Crawford arrived on the Tuesday morning, but that evening he accidentally discovered there were from thirty to forty camped in the horse paddock, about half a mile from the station. Mr. Crawford and his party charged their camp and found Mr. V. S. Scott's saddle and bridle and some other things[47].

In nineteenth-century parlance, words such as 'charged their camp,' 'dispersed them,' 'taught them a lesson' or even 'have a picnic with the natives' all meant one thing – massacre. The Newcastle University concluded that Crawford killed thirty or more men, women, and children in this revenge expedition, and a few days later, Browne and his party managed to get thirty or so more.

Interviewed after his time at VRD about his relationships with the local tribes, Crawford recalled:

> During the last 10 years, in fact, since first white man settled

here, we've held no communication with the natives at all,
except with the rifle. They've never been allowed near this
station or the outstations, being too treacherous and warlike[48].

Crawford managed VRD until 1894, when he relinquished
his position to the infamous Jack Watson. He then worked with
Hildebrand Stevens, shipping live cattle to Java and Singapore, until
that trade was destroyed by the tick borne Redwater Fever.

After that he returned to work on the Overland Telegraph
Line, joining Alfred Pybus in a telegraph maintenance party, but
when Pybus died and was buried at Powell Creek Telegraph Station
in 1898, Crawford took over as manager until his own death, near
Newcastle Waters, from dysentery, in 1901. He was a resident of the
Territory for decades, and had seen some tough times, but his death
was apparently "brought on by exposure during the recent heavy
rains"[49].

Crawford was 48 years old, a bachelor all his life, and was much
respected by the white settlers of the Northern Territory. One postscript on his life is worth telling. In 1884, four copper miners were
murdered near Burrundie, 200 km south of Darwin, by Woolwonga
people. The retribution by several parties against the tribe was terrible[50]
and for many years it was believed that the Woolwonga tribe been

Figure 7: Lindsay Crawford's grave lies in the bush, north of Newcastle Waters (photo:
Eddie Webber).

wiped out. Then, in 2009, someone looked closely at *Thompson's List of Half Castes in 1899*[51], and one of the children listed was a ten-year-old named May, whose mother was Jennie of the Woolwonga tribe.

May had been given the name of her father, Crawford. She grew up to have five children[52] of her own, and their descendants, many of whom live in Darwin, now know their family's history. They live with the tragedy of their ancestors[53], and the knowledge that their family is the last of the Woolwonga tribe.

Jack Watson

Figure 8: Jack Watson (1890, Anon - Cruikshank collection, 95271318).

One cattleman who became infamous for the severity of his interactions with the local tribes was Jack (John) Watson. Born in 1852 to a wealthy Irish immigrant family living in Melbourne, Watson had a charmed childhood. He excelled at all sports at Melbourne Grammar School, became captain of the rowing team, and a champion rifle shot. His father was a well-known business and sport identity throughout Victoria, including, for several years, as the starter of the Melbourne Cup.

In his twenties, Jack Watson moved to Queensland to work with a brother, William Henry, who managed Currawilla Station. Here, he learned to shoot matchboxes off the heads of his Aboriginal stockmen. Jack was soon employed as a manager at Lawn Hill Station, owned by Frank Hann. Emily Creaghe visited him here in 1883 and noted 40 pairs of Aboriginal ears nailed to wall of the shed. Watson and Hann were probably responsible for many other Aboriginal deaths as well. The local Native Police, led by Sub-Inspector James Lamond, shot over 100 men, women, and children on Lawn Hill alone[54].

Watson soon took up droving, taking a mob to stock McArthur River Station over the border. On his return he met Charlie Gaunt and his droving party, who had been attacked by Aboriginal people. Several of their horses had been speared, but none of the cattlemen was injured. Outraged, Watson chose to mount a punitive expedition. Gaunt recalled the story in 1934:

> … There were himself and four first class blackboys. We told him what happened. "Leave them to me," said Jack. "I'll stir the possum in them when I get to Skeleton Creek," and he did. Spending two weeks on the creek he tracked and hunted those niggers, shooting them down as he came up with them until there was not a black on the creek. He was merciless and spared none[55].

Gaunt seemed to be in awe of Watson.

> … Jack was a wild reckless fellow. He would charge hell with a bucket of water. A splendid athlete and boxer, good bushman and stockman and a terror on the blacks[56].

When Watson moved to the Northern Territory in 1886, he brought the Queensland model of dealing with the Aboriginal tribes with him. He worked for Alexandria Station for a couple of years, then transferred to Florida Station in Arnhem Land, on Yolngu country near today's town of Ramingining. Aboriginal resistance here had been high since the station was established by John Macartney in 1885. In fact, the first manager, Jim Randall, had thought it necessary to mount a swivel cannon on his veranda for defense. When Watson took over management in 1889, however, he was much more aggressive. He mounted hunting expeditions and:

> … threw the lead at them and threw it to kill. He had the blacks of Blue Mud and Caledon Bays good hombres, but he had to wipe out a lot to make them so. In all the early days of Florida there was not a white man attacked or killed by blacks. The men of Florida knew how to handle blacks…[57]

There are stories told in Ramingining and Milingimbi about children climbing trees to escape white men on horses, before being shot by them and falling to the ground.

When Florida Station closed in 1892, Macartney employed Watson to move the station equipment and drive the cattle to Auvergne Station, near the Territory's western border.

After Sam Croker, the manager of Auvergne, was murdered by Charlie Flannigan[58], Watson took over, but he only stayed there a year. In March 1895, he took over Victoria River Downs Station from Lindsay Crawford. His reputation preceded him, and all the Aboriginal workers on the station are said to have run away, including his own 'servant,' a man named Pompey. When Pompey was killed, Watson asked the local policeman, the notorious Mounted Constable William Willshire, to bring him Pompey's skull for use as a spittoon. Willshire complied[59].

The Durack Family

Visitors to the East Kimberley region and Kununurra won't travel far before hearing the name of Durack. Many will tour the Duracks' 1895 Argyle Homestead museum which, like the ancient Egyptian temple of Abu Simbal, was dismantled brick by brick and transported to higher ground after the Ord River was dammed in 1971 and Lake Argyle began to fill.

Figure 9: Patrick Durack (1834-1898) (ABH).

The Durack family was a force in the Kimberley for many years. The family had originally settled around Goulburn in New South Wales in the 1850s, after immigrating from Ireland. Brothers Patrick 'Patsy' and Michael Durack were the first to head north, leaving New South Wales in 1879. They drove 7,250 breeding cattle and two hundred horses across the continent to the Kimberley, and established

Carlton Hill and Ivanhoe Stations in 1882. Their 4,800-kilometre journey of cattle remains a droving record, rivalled only by that of the MacDonald brothers, to Fossil Downs, two years later.

In 1883, Patsy Durack and Tom Kilfoyle took sheep from the Cambridge Gulf westward across the Kimberley, following Forrest's exploration route. They reported favourably on the country they passed. Their sheep remained in good condition throughout and this was a great relief to the colony, reported the *West Australian*, because if they had:

> … been dissatisfied and reported adversely, the value of
> Kimberley leases would have fallen very low; it is therefore
> with very great pleasure that we are able to announce that
> Mr. Durack and his party bring us a satisfactory report of this
> portion of our territory[60].

Durack then planned to bring 20,000 more sheep to the Kimberley overland, but cattle began to prove more successful, and this huge drive never happened.

Some of the family's success in the Kimberley came down to the luck of being in the right place at the right time. The Halls Creek gold rush, for example, occurred just as the they had cattle to sell. Patsy's 21-year-old brother, Michael Durack[61], known as 'M.P.', made a major sale to a Halls Creek butcher on 22 July 1886, his 21st birthday. The cattle were mustered and sold for £1200 of 'raw gold' – in today's dollars about $350,000. Mary Durack recorded that he sold "7PD[62] [branded] bullocks at £17 a head and cows at £15"[63].

M.P. was helped in the setting up of Argyle Station by his young brother, 'Big Johnny'. Unfortunately for the family, John did not survive for long:

> … It appears that Mr. John Durack was cattle hunting 50
> miles from his station when he suddenly came upon a mob
> of natives. He had just time to call out to the boy who was
> following him: " Look out, there are a lot of natives here with
> spears" when he received a spear through his body. He set
> spurs to is horse and galloped eighty yards when he fell off his
> saddle and died immediately. The boy who accompanied him

[his brother] hastened to the station and returned with the deceased's brothers and found that the body had been riddled with spears after death[64].

The white settlers were not going to put up with the murder of one of their own, particularly one of the Durack family. A party of police was led by Augustus Lucanus, who was another mass-killer. He learned how to kill while working in the Northern Territory, and had long experience of retribution expeditions, against the people he called 'the niggers':

> … left Wyndham on the 28th inst., accompanied by Mr.
> M. Durack with the object of tracing up and bringing to
> justice the offenders. The party will be reinforced at Messrs.
> Durack's station and will number sixteen strong all told. This
> I am afraid is the beginning of troubles with the natives.
> The natives, judging from reports, appear to be very fearless
> and when they are more accustomed to the whites we shall
> probably have many cases of native depredations, cattle
> stealing, spearing, etc[65].

The Territory newspapers took up the story, baying for revenge:

> A party went out from the station to find and bury the
> deceased; they found that the body had been jobbed full of
> spear holes, quite 80 or 90 holes having been made; they
> also found some stone spear heads under the body. From the
> tracks, it was estimated that there must have been 70 or 80
> natives in the party. The horses, saddles, and packs were found
> untouched near the body.
>
> The Sergeant of Police and a body of troopers, with volunteers,
> have gone out in pursuit, and we hope that they will give a
> good account of the murderers, undeterred by any fears of a
> Western Australian "Parson Wott" or his prototype Gribble, or
> any other of the white-chokered fraternity.[66]

And a few days later:

> A party of six troopers has been sent out in search of the
> murderers of the late John Durack. Another party, including
> the unfortunate man's brothers and several other Europeans
> has also started after the offending tribe. We trust they will
> find them and administer a lesson such as will not be soon
> forgotten[67].

Massacre researcher Chris Owen concluded that the biggest revenge massacre in Western Australia followed the death of Big Johnny. Hundreds were killed by Augustus Lucanus and his party. They "rounded about 120 natives up, and shot a large number consisting of men, women and children"[68, 69].

Waterloo Station, across the border in the Northern Territory, is said to have been named after the famous battle and, as Lewis puts it, the "unrestrained slaughter" of local Aboriginals by police after the spearing of 'Big Johnny' Durack in 1886.

Cattleman Doug Moore's 'boy', Jerry, was an eyewitness who hid in an ant bed during the slaughter and escaped in the dark. He claimed the shooting only stopped when the ammunition ran out[70]. A further 110 people are said to have died in this massacre.

The scale of the murders is hard to fathom, even to relatives of the perpetrators. For instance, Mary Durack in *Kings in Grass Castles*, claimed the revenge party were led on a four-day wild goose chase, before giving up the hunt in some lonely limestone range. She concluded everything else was rumour:

> The conspiracy of silence that sealed the lips of the pioneers
> added colour to the rumours that spread abroad so that
> whereas we know they took much rough justice into their own
> hands they were no doubt less devastating to the local tribes
> than was sometimes said. 'Punitive expeditions,' like brumby
> musters, took a great deal of time and organisation and in that
> wild land where ranges and impenetrable gorges formed so
> ideal a refuge for fugitives they returned from such projects, as
> often as not, completely defeated[71].

But in an oral history collected from Jack Banggaiyerri Sullivan there is a version that puts Big Johnnie Durack in another light. It led Chris Owen to conclude that the cause of the original murder seemed to rest with John Durack himself.

"Big Johnny was just shooting everything that moved," he was told:

... When they started forming the stations, Johnnie Durack

would ride around from the old station with a pack, round and round to find the good places. One day he was in the lead while another fella drove his pack, and he put down to where he was going to cross a creek. That was where he ran into the blackfellers. Instead of frightening them away he straightaway pulled out a gun – bang bang bang bang – and chased one feller down to the creek. The blackfeller ducked around and as Johnnie passed him, looking out for him, of course he let drive from the side and got him. When his mate found out he was speared he just galloped away leaving the pack horses there. If he had let the blackfellers go it would not have happened, but they all had the bloody wind up"[72].

Not all the Duracks appear to have been so trigger happy – but then, as Mary said, their lips were sealed.

Overlanders

Travellers, who were called 'overlanders' by the press, moved across the Territory then, as now, and tended to travel the same routes. The Overland Telegraph Line, or OTL, that ran between Port Augusta and Port Darwin was the busiest route but tracks also came and went between Queensland and Western Australia.

In the vast distances, wayside inns, sly grog shanties, and supply stores were soon built, particularly around and between the telegraph stations, and along the most-used tracks through the bush. South of Port Darwin, for example, there were sly-grog shanties, or 'hotels', at 12-Mile, Stapleton, Bridge Creek, Yam Creek, Adelaide River, Pine Creek, Katherine, Elsey, Abraham's Billabong, Anthony's Lagoon, Roper Bar, Timber Creek, and many others.

Overland routes were well publicised in the newspapers. For example, Tom Kilfoyle, of the Ord, informed his readers that getting to the Kimberley from Katherine in the Territory was possible overland:

> … If travelling by land from the Katherine, the distance would be about 580 miles, and a good road. Furthest stage without water, 20 miles[73].

During the busy months of the rush to the Kimberley in 1886, the roadside hotels and sly-grog establishments were well known, and essential for the well-being of the travellers. They were places where travellers drank and dined, and drank some more, preparing themselves for the next stage overland.

There was always grog. Rum was more important to many people than food, and it would be rafted across flooded rivers instead of flour. Grog was carted to sly-grog shanties that bore evocative names like 'Devil's Delight' and 'Beggar's Retreat' – and it could be deadly. For example, in the 1870s, Fannie Nicholas's death was recorded as being from "excessive drinking" at Union Reef, and Edwin Allan, a miner, died of "exposure to the sun after excessive drinking" when he fell asleep in the sun on the banks of the Adelaide River[74].

When the real stuff ran out, publicans made their own: 'Sunset Rum,' for instance, was a mix of methylated spirits and kerosene, with Worcestershire sauce, ginger, and sugar.

Overlanders rested their horses and camped close to these shanties – sometimes for months. In December 1886, the *North Australian* reported that there were "30 or 40 overlanders camped [in Katherine], bound for Kimberley, but waiting for provisions"[75].

Most of these men were heading to the goldfields at Halls Creek, but others were cattlemen or shepherds, looking for work on the remote stations of the north as the cattle industry expanded. The managers of the stations and the 'boss drovers' who delivered their cattle, became household names across the north. Mary Durack called them "Kings in Grass Castles".

For talented horsemen, used to life in the bush, there was always work to be had somewhere, though gold fever does funny things to people. In desperate haste to reach the goldfields, some men would shuck off their normal persona and morals and participate in events that were uncharacteristic. One such man was Tom Nugent, who would find himself the leader of a gang of larrikin bushrangers.

Thomas Nugent and his Mates

Figure 10: Tom Nugent (c 1900, SLSA B-38780).

Born to James and Ellen (nee Harrington) in March 1848[76], Thomas Harrington O'Brien Nugent was one of ten siblings. He started his cattle work as a young man. He may have worked on a cattle drive from Elderslie (near Camden in New South Wales) taking cattle northwards towards the Northern Territory in 1870. If this is true, this trip already imbeds him in history, as this drive was one of the earliest into the Northern Territory.

By 1873, the 25-year-old may have been back near his hometown, because a Thomas Nugent reported that his mare was stolen near Gulgong. The next year he was in Queensland, working as a horse-breaker in Rockhampton. By 1876, he was the head stockman on Welltown Station, near Toowoomba[77], and by the time he was thirty, he was a boss drover, moving large numbers of cattle through the open country of Southern Queensland. As *The Maitland Mercury* reported:

> Mr Thomas Nugent, in charge of 1300 head of cattle
> belonging to Mr. Clynes, of Talwood, passed through Surat on
> the way to the Diamantina[78].

Moving west into the Territory, he helped start a new cattle station southwest of Camooweal near Lake Nash, for John Costello[79]. He then became head stockman on another new station, named Carandotta, near Boulia on the Georgina River in 1884.

The next year he was working near Renner Springs, in the Northern Territory, some 20 km north of the country he would later lease, to begin his own cattle station. At some time during these years, he also worked at Brunette Downs, with Harry Redford as the manager. They may therefore have been firm friends and travelled together in the early 1880s, sharing many nights under the stars on the plains.

Some of this timeline is guesswork, but one thing is clear: by the mid-1880s, Nugent was an expert horseman and cattleman, with bush survival skills for which he would become famous. And with mateship from a kindred spirit like Harry Redford, whose transgressions of the law hampered him not at all, where else would Nugent have gone to follow his dreams, other than the sunlit plains of the remotest parts of the vast inland of Australia?

It was there that Nugent heard the stories of the fist-sized gold nuggets waiting to be picked up on the newly discovered Halls Creek goldfield, in the Kimberley of Western Australia. If Hall and Slattery could find a 28-ounce nugget, why not he?

He wasn't the only one listening to the stories of easy riches. Suddenly, the horse pads, and the cart and wheelbarrow tracks, were overtaken by hundreds of dirt-poor hopefuls, with gold-dust in their eyes. Nugent worked his way north, along the track that ran beside the Overland Telegraph Line, most likely directly from Eva Downs Station, which he managed at the time[80]. Very quickly, he found a bunch of mates to travel with[81], meeting them either at Renner Springs[82], Johnstons Waterhole[83], or at Powell Creek Telegraph Station.

The most well-known of these mates was Alexander 'Sandy Myrtle' MacDonald. Prior to 1886, MacDonald worked on a sheep station named Myrtle Springs, near Farina[84], a small town north of the Flinders Ranges in South Australia. In 1882, and known as Government Gums, Farina was as far as you could go by train in South Australia[85], and the rails crossed Myrtle Springs. The station's wool was therefore easily transported to Port Augusta by rail. The country there is marginal, and the droughts of the late 1860s and the floods that followed them, destroyed many thousands of sheep.

In early 1886, MacDonald heard the stories of 28-ounce nuggets lying in the ground of the East Kimberley, ready for collection. Accepting his 'gold fever,' he resigned his post, and set off, first to Marree, and then northwest, skirting the southern end of Lake Eyre. In the flat South Australian landscape, stretching across the state for hundreds of kilometres, freshwater comes from mound springs. These occur where artesian water continually seeps to the surface and has for so long, that deposits of sediments have grown to become high mounds. Before sheep and cattle arrived to trample them, these sensitive systems were soft and metres high, and they were obvious places for pastoralists to locate their homesteads – and for Charles Todd to build the telegraph stations. MacDonald spent days following the line, and riding from one mound spring to the next. At Strangways, The Peake, and at Oodnadatta, MacDonald could refill his water bags easily. After that, from Neales Creek on the outskirts of the town of Oodnadatta, he needed to cross an 80-kilometre dry stage on the way to Charlotte Waters.

He probably was rarely alone. Everyone travelled along the track that ran beside the Overland Telegraph Line, and it was wise for individuals to join up with their fellow travellers. MacDonald quickly fell in with several men who would soon join him in notoriety. There is no record of where or when they met, but they were all at a race meeting together in Alice Springs and left there as a group.

Initially, there were five others: Hugh 'Scottie' Campbell, a Scottish sailor and talented pugilist who had recently jumped ship in Port Augusta: Jack Dalley, a drover and farmer from near the South Australian town of Terowie; 'Wonoka'[86] Jack Brown and George Brown, two brothers from Hawker in South Australia; and James Woodford, also from South Australia.

In mid-1886, somewhere along the road[87], the South Australians linked up with some Queenslanders: 'Larrikin Bill' Smith, a cattleman from Normanton in the Gulf region; Bob Anderson, another cattleman; Jim Woodroffe Fitzgerald; and the youngest member to join the group, 'Tommy the Rag', who was to be the most successful of the gang in keeping his identity secret.

Queenslanders all, these men travelled from their homes to the Northern Territory. They may have already been travelling together, or with others, and it is possible that they were perfectly innocent of any crimes at the time they met. However, it is also possible that they were already horse thieves. Many Queenslanders stole horses before riding to the Territory:

> HORSE STEALERS have been both numerous and daring
> of late, and although the police have been out repeatedly in
> pursuit they have not succeeded in a solitary capture. The
> boundary line between the two colonies being so close at hand
> is very convenient for bush criminals[88].

Whatever their history, each of them was in the Territory at the right time to become a part of the Ragged Thirteen.

The twelfth man was from New South Wales. He was gold-crazy 'New England' Jack Woods, who would make a habit of following any new rush across Australia, before eventually returning to his family in Armidale.

The thirteenth man to join them was a New Zealander who was already living in the Territory, named Jim Carmody. Carmody was brother-in-law to a smuggler well-known in Borroloola and the northern community, 'Māori Jack' Reid. This notorious man, as we shall see, played a significant role in forging the gang together.

Using nicknames or pseudonyms helped the gang remain anonymous. Tom Nugent called himself Tom Holmes, and Alexander MacDonald used Sandy Myrtle. The name 'Tommy the Rag' appears nowhere else, except erroneously in several mid-twentieth century newspapers as 'Jimmy the Rag'. It may also have been Tommy the *Lag* at one time, suggesting that Tommy may have been an ex-prisoner.

The gang avoided publicity and never faced a court of law. None of them was ever gaoled for their offences and none, in the following decades, was happy to talk about their time in the gang – at least, when sober. When they broke up, they drifted to other parts of the country and 'went straight'. Records of most of them are as scanty as rumours about them were rife.

They were travelling companions who became a 'gang' of bushrangers when they became united in crime. Their criminal career began at a lonely bush pub and store that stood on the stock route close to Elsey Station, and near enough to Abraham's Billabong[89] to hear the crocodiles cough at night.

Endnotes

1 Named the 'Northern Territory of South Australia' from 1862 to 1911.

2 Rose, 1964.

3 Brothers and sub-inspectors of the Queensland Native Police, Reg and D'Arcy Uhr's history is one of killings, kidnapping of women and young children, and the near total breakdown of the traditional tribal groups in the areas they patrolled, based around Burketown. The *Port Dennison Times* reported on 4 June 1868, "everybody in the district is delighted with the wholesale slaughter dealt out by the native police". The newspaper thanked those involved in "ridding the district of fifty-nine myalls" in 1869 (in Reynolds 1989). Uhr died of appendicitis in 1907, without ever answering for his behaviour. For the full horrific history of the Queensland Native Police, see Marr 2023.

4 James Barry, quoted in Marr, *Killing for Country*, p 366

5 Bowerlee Station was named after the Government Resident's horse.

6 On 13 April 1874, Cox fought with his nephew, Charles Bourchier, who stabbed him in his side. Bourchier was charged with assault, taken to court, and fined five pounds. In disgrace, he left the Northern Territory and got away with murder, because Cox soon died from his wound (see Pugh, 2021).

7 George de Latour, like Uhr, was another mass-killer of Aboriginal people. He and his son were both murdered in the New Hebrides in 1913, and 'the body of the son was taken away and eaten, amidst great rejoicing' (*Sydney Morning Herald*, 13 October 1913).

8 Glencoe Station was 5,900 km² lease that is now called Delamere Station.

9 As Glencoe Station was relatively close to Yam Creek and the goldfields, it had a ready market for any meat produced.

10 Alfred's wife, Mary, was the first woman to settle on a pastoral property in the Norther Territory (James, 1995).

11 Cross, 2011.

12 Elsey Station became famous across the globe to readers of Jeannie Gunn's *We of the Never Never.*

13 Robbery Under Arms (1888) by Thomas Alexander Browne, AKA Rolf Boldrewood.

14 The real 'Captain Starlight' was a nasty bushranger named Frank Pearson (1837-99) who operated in western New South Wales and spent much of his adult life in prison.

15 The traditional lands of the Iningai people of Central Queensland spread about 52,000 km² in the region that now includes the towns of Longreach, Muttaburra, and Aramac.

16 Mary Durack (1959) *Kings of Grass Castles*. John Costello subsequently opened up the Strzelecki track legitimately

17 *Queenslander*, Saturday 22 February 1873, page 10.

18 Mary Durack (1959) claimed it was a '500 guineas bull'.

19 Elvey also appears later in the story, thousands of kilometres away, in the first days

of settlement at Wyndham.

20 Blanchwater Station lies near Lake Callabonna, S.A., 236 km southwest of Innamincka.

21 *Brisbane Courier,* Tuesday 17 June 1873, page 3.

22 *Sydney Morning Herald*, Saturday 1 March 1873, page 5.

23 Charles W. Blakeney, Judge of the Western District Court, to the Honourable John Bramston, the Attorney General Crown Law-offices, Brisbane, 22nd March 1873. Some members of the jury were also in disagreement. This from five of them: 'Sir – We, the undersigned jurors of the Western District Court of Queensland, having been present at the trial of Regina v Redford, desire to express in the strongest manner our surprise and indignation at the verdict given in that trial, and we consider that a more disgraceful miscarriage of justice never took place in any court of law. And we further consider that it is perfectly useless to bring cases of cattle stealing before this Court at Roma unless the present jury list be very much altered' (*Brisbane Courier*,17 June 1873, page 3).

24 *Northern Territory Times and Gazette,* 27 February 1874.

25 *Northern Territory Times and Gazette*, 1 September 1883.

26 *Observer*, 6 October 1883.

27 In Gaunt's version of the story, Giles was rescued by his Aboriginal 'wife', a woman named Kitty, who brought water back to him in her cap. Tom Nugent also appears in Gaunt's story, when 'some years later' the pair discovered the bones of two of the party and their horses, still with their saddles on. Gaunt also claimed that Shirley had 'blown his brains out' rather than die of thirst (*Northern Standard,* 2 October 1931)

28 M.C. John Shirley was 27 years old. The Police Association of South Australia say he was the first policeman to die in the line of duty in the Northern Territory.

29 *Chronicle*, 23 February 1884.

30 Extracts from Mr Little's Diary, *Northern Territory Times and Gazette*, 16 March 1900, page 3.

31 Linklater and Tapp, 1968.

32 Nat Buchanan (1826-1901) died on Walcha N.S.W. in 1901. His grace is well signposted for interested travellers.

33 *Norther Standard* (Darwin) 22 January 1931, page 5.

34 *West Australian* (Perth, WA), 7 September 1937, page 12.

35 The pioneers of Ord River station and the East Kimberleys were Bob Button, manager, Paddy MacDonald, G.W. Campbell, Octolonius Turtle Sinclair, and Donald Swan. *West Australian*, 7 September 1937, page 12.

36 Clement & Bridge (Ed.), *Kimberley Scenes by D. Swan*, 1991.

37 Swan, in Clement and Bridge, 1991.

38 Creaghe, 1883.

39 The first edition of *The Northern Territory Times*, published on 7 November 1873, announced 'the manufacture of good drinks for the people of North Australia is now, thanks to Mr. Crawford, becoming an established fact. Lemonade, soda water, and ginger beer are being turned out in first-rate style; and what is more,

Mr. Crawford is about to begin brewing good malt liquors, a matter in which he is sanguine of success'. It did not last, however. By January the next year E.J.F. Crawford was 'obliged, on account of ill-health, to return to Melbourne' (*Northern Territory Times and Gazette*, 9 January 1874, page 2). Lindsay chose to stay in Port Darwin. He appears often in lists of the cricket team and other sports.

40 Creaghe, 1883.

41 Creaghe, 1883.

42 Creaghe, 1883.

43 Croker was later murdered by Charlie Flannigan at Auvergne Station. Flannigan was the first man to be legally hung in the N.T. for his crime (see Christopherson 2023)

44 Lewis, 2004.

45 Willeroo Station lies on the Victoria Highway, west of Katherine N.T., north of Victoria River Downs and Delamere. Crawford and Scott were neighbours.

46 *Northern Territory Times and Gazette*, 4 November 1892, page 3.

47 *Northern Territory Times and Gazette,* 11 Nov 1892, Page 3, The Willeroo Tragedy

48 See Smith 2024.

49 *Advertiser*, 21 March 1901, page 4.

50 Pugh, 2021, Smith, 2024.

51 *Thompson's List of Half Castes in the Northern Territory 1899*. LANT.

52 Martin Calma 1905-1955, Juana Calma 1908-1954, plus Johan, Maurice and Felmina, who may have died in infancy.

53 Purtill, 2014.

54 Roberts, (2005).

55 *Northern Standard* (Darwin), 6 July 1934, page 4: The Lepers Of Arnheim Land And Sketches.

56 *Northern Standard* (Darwin), 6 July 1934, page 4: The Lepers Of Arnheim Land And Sketches.

57 *Northern Standard* (Darwin), 6 July 1934, page 4: The Lepers Of Arnheim Land And Sketches.

58 See Pugh, 2023. Flannigan was the first person in the Territory to be legally executed. See also Christophersen 2023.

59 Lewis, 2012.

60 *West Australian*, 5 January 1883, page 3, Trip of Mr. Durack and Party across Kimberley.

61 M.P. was the father of Dame Mary Durack, author of *Kings in Grass Castles*.

62 '7PD' was Patsy Durack's brand. Seven was his lucky number, and PD were his initials.

63 Mary Durack, 1959.

64 *Western Mail*, 25 December 1886, page 11: *Wyndham Notes*.

65 *Western Mail*, 25 December 1886, page 11: *Wyndham Notes*.

66 *Northern Territory Times and Gazette,* 11 December 1886, page 3.

67 *Northern Territory Times and Gazette,* 25 December 1886, page 2.

68 Owen (2016). See also *The West Australian*, November 14, 1892, page 3, and Smith,

2024.

69 https://c21ch.newcastle.edu.au/colonialmassacres.

70 Lewis, 2021, pp 527-528.

71 Mary Durack, (1959), (1986 Corgi reprint, page 300)

72 Shaw, B (ed) 1983(a), *Banggaiyerri, The Story of Jack Sullivan as told to Bruce Shaw*, AIATSIS, Canberra. Quoted by Newcastle University.

73 *Northern Territory Times and Gazette*, 12 June 1886, page 3

74 Register of Deaths, 1870s, LANT.

75 *North Australian*, 10 December 1886, page 3.

76 James Nugent was the innkeeper of the Gordon Arms in Lochinvar (N.S.W.) and he and Ellen had ten children. Little more is known about the Nugent family from those days, but James died in Maitland in 1859, when Tom was eleven years old, and his estate was declared insolvent with a deficit of £133 15.s. 6d. It must have been tough for Ellen to raise the family.

77 *Telegraph* (Brisbane), 15 March 1876, page 6.

78 *The Maitland Mercury and Hunter River General Advertiser*, 17 August 1878, page 14.

79 *Australian Star* (Sydney), 29 October 1907, page 5.

80 Gaunt says he and Nugent left Eva Downs Station at about the same time (Charles Gaunt, *Northern Standard*, 18 September 1931, page 4: Old Time Memories). Eva Downs Station is on the Barkly Tablelands, about 300 km northeast of Tennant Creek.

81 Dozens of wannabes claimed membership of the Ragged Thirteen, and some of them are mentioned in these pages. William ('Billy Miller') Linklater provided what appears to be the most accurate list of the original membership. He was a stockman who worked for Tom Nugent at Banka Banka, long after the gang split up. He listed: Tom Nugent, Sandy Myrtle, Larrikin Bill Smith, Jim Fitzgerald, Bob Anderson, Hugh Campbell, Tommy the Rag, "Wonoka" Jack Brown, George Brown, "New England" Jack Woods, Jim Carmody, Jack Dalley, and Jimmy Woodford (Linklater and Tapp, 1997).

82 Ernestine Hill, 1951.

83 Nat Buchanan may have met them camped at Johnstons Waterhole, near Frews Ponds, about 600km south of Darwin.

84 Myrtle Springs Station was owned by Alexander Borthwick Murray in partnership with George Tinline. It spread over 890 km² and had a potential carrying capacity (in good years) of 29,000 sheep. It is about 60 km south of Marree.

85 The railway line was extended to Marree (Hergott Springs) in 1884, and to Oodnadatta in 1890.

86 The nickname *Wonoka* comes from Wonoka Station. The town of Hawker is on the station's boundary. It is likely that Jack and George Brown were shepherds or at least workers on the station, perhaps sawyers, prior to their travel north.

87 Ernestine Hill suggests they met at Renner Springs, but for travellers coming in from the East, from Borroloola for instance, it is likely they would meet the Overland Telegraph Line at Powell Creek, Frews Ironstone Ponds, or Daly Waters,

which are all north of Renner Springs. Johnstons Waterhole, where Buchanan may have met them, is also near Frews Ironstone Ponds, about 600km south of Darwin.

88 *Brisbane Courier,* 14 January 1885, page 6: Burketown.

89 Abraham's Billabong was named by Stephen King in 1872, after a labourer on John Ross's Overland Telegraph Line exploration party.

Chapter 2
The Ragged Thirteen

Abraham's Billabong

Abraham's Billabong is a large, picturesque stretch of water that lies about three kilometres northeast of the modern town of Mataranka – a town well-known to travellers because the warm waters of Mataranka Thermal Pools and Bitter Springs are highly attractive modern destinations. The billabong, however, is on private land and is now rarely visited. In the 1880s, as indeed now, many travellers camped near the springs to frolic in the clear warm waters beneath huge fan palms[1]. Abraham's Billabong store was just a short walk through the bush. It was, as the *North Australian* informed everyone, newly built in 1884:

> M'Phee [sic] and Co's, store at Abraham's Billabong is rapidly nearing completion. The position is central for the overland traffic, and I have every reason to believe that this most welcome venture will be a very great success[2].

It became a well-known stop on the overland cattle route. At just eighty-nine miles from the Katherine River, it was a "great convenience to overlanders." The 'goods supplier' who opened it in February 1885[3], Bob McPhee, caught gold fever a few months later and set off for Halls Creek in October 1885[4], so the licence was transferred, but to whom is confusing. The *Times* reported that William Hay had purchased the store in 1885, but he did not own it for long. By 1886, it was owned by M.D. Armstrong and Adam Bryden, who

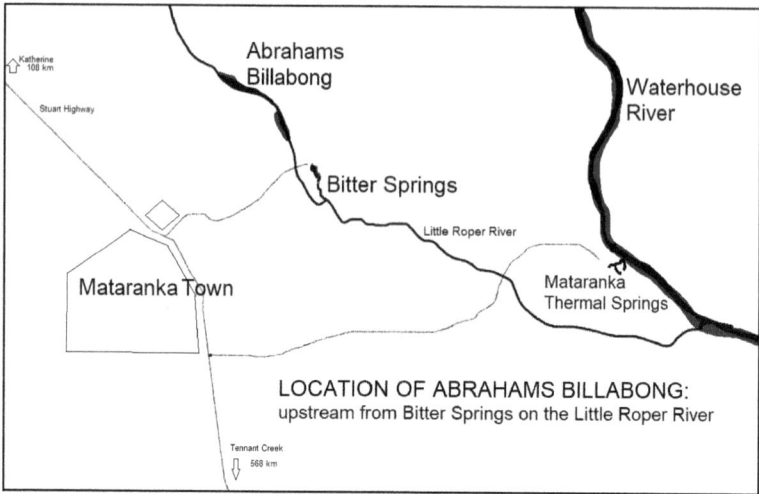

Map 1: Location of Abraham's Billabong.

were already the owners of the Roper Bar Hotel. For some unknown reason, Armstrong was refused a licence for the Abraham's Billabong store in 1886[5], but it continued to operate anyway.

Matthew Kirwin[6], a man who held a reputation for being a fighter, was granted a storekeeper's licence to run the store at Roper Bar in 1884[7], and later at Abraham's Billabong in 1887[8]. It seems likely that Kirwin worked for Armstrong and Bryden[9], as the newspapers stated, but he may have owned nothing other than the licences.

The busy stock routes of the 1880s naturally presented opportunities for men willing to operate in the service industries, like Kirwin. His ability to fight was a quality well-suited to storekeeping. In a time when most of the customers were rough and ready, hard-drinking cattlemen, some of whom were willing to pay for the grog and supplies with dodgy cheques, an ability and readiness to fight for correct payment must have come in useful.

The stores were not grand affairs. Surveyor David Lindsay visited Abraham's Billabong in 1888 and was not impressed. It was, he wrote, a:

> … solitary hut—a store. How the owner manages to make
> a living is a mystery, although his life is to not altogether

uneventful. During the rush to the Kimberley the monotony of his life was broken by travellers[10].

Of course, it was the travelling stockmen who brought the owners most of their income. In those years, all the large cattle drives that crossed the Northern Territory, destined both for Territory stations and the Kimberley, passed along the same stock routes. It was therefore easy to find customers for supplies for the stock camps, and, of course, grog.

Also, in December or January of each year, many thousands of cattle were settled down for the wet season, and men would often camp near the wayside stores:

> CATTLE are still continuing to pour into the Territory and its immediate neighborhood west. I hear from a party just arrived from Queensland that there are 30,000 head between Burketown and the Roper, 5000 being for the McArthur River, 16,000 for Western Australia, and a lot for Powells Creek and other places. Durack's cattle will camp at Rosie Creek for the wet season. This mob comprises 3000 head breeding cattle and are bound for the Ord River. 1100 head of cattle, the property of Fisher and Lyons, are leaving the Roper for the Victoria River in a few days, Anderson in charge. These are cattle mustered by Mr. W. Hay, that were lost from mobs travelling through from Queensland. Craigh [sic: Creagh], who came over with Mr. E. Favenc last year, has brought cattle over to stock the Hodson and Burdan country[11].

After the wet season, the cattle began moving again. In May 1885, the news from Abraham's Billabong was that:

> … Mr Galloway is here with Cooper's cattle and intends going a short cut to the Victoria; Cooper also goes with the cattle. Durack Bros. will be here today with 2,000 head for the Ord River, and there are three mobs just behind Messrs. Durack's. The distance from here to the Victoria is about 110 miles, and a good distance is saved by not going to the Katherine[12].

Other overlanders on the road between Abraham's Billabong and Katherine included wannabe miners from South Australia and Queensland. They passed through in ever increasing numbers in

1886 and 1887. The Times mentioned them in August:

> Overlanders are still passing the Katherine in numbers
> bound for the Kimberley; a number are reported as camped
> at the billabong recruiting their horses on young grass, and
> themselves on fresh milk[13].

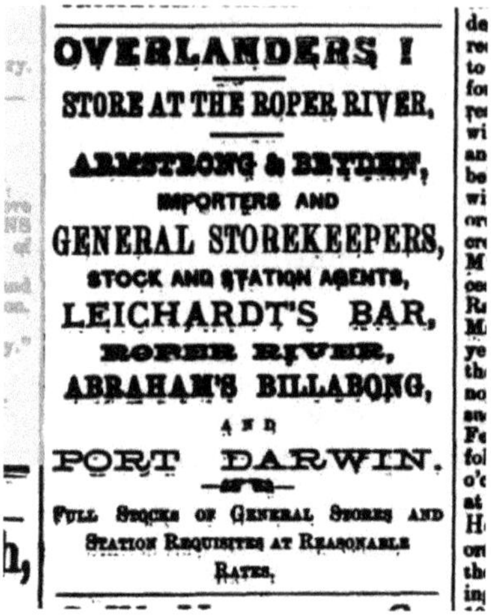

Figure 11: Abraham's Billabong Store, as advertised in the *Northern Territory Times* and *Gazette* on 22 Jan 1887.

By September 1886, the *North Australian* reported that 'Armstrong & Bryden have been doing a grand trade at Abraham's Billabong among the overlanders'[14], despite Armstrong not having a licence[15].

A few months later Mat Kirwin visited Abraham's Billabong from Roper Bar, perhaps in preparation for taking over. The store was then managed by a young man named Bowen, who was running a fine trade with the overlanders camped nearby. One of them was Charles Gaunt, who wrote his memories, decades later, of the events that took place.

Bowen was a 'tenderfoot, inexperienced and soft pie'[16], he said, who may have been unprepared to manage the group of twelve men who unsaddled their horses and set up camp at Bitter Springs in August or September of that year.

The twelve were not, at first sight, an unusual group of travellers for those times, and once their horses were seen to, and their camp marked out, the men walked the short distance up the Little Roper River to Abraham's Billabong for a drink. Gin, schnapps, and especially rum were readily transported throughout the bush in thick black bottles known as 'squares,' and clearly there was a good supply ready and waiting for them.

Time passed and the drinkers were soon merry – and destructive.

Furniture and fittings were broken in their drunken glee as Bowen lost control of the mob. Worse, he failed to recognise the cheques, that they were happily using to pay for their grog, were duds. "What a harvest they reaped with those crooked cheques" wrote Gaunt:

> [Bowen] took them like a baby takes mother's milk and did a roaring trade, the crowd bringing the cheques into him by handfuls[17].

Gaunt says that Mat Kirwin tried to quell the forthcoming trouble. He took Bowen 'to task, for taking unknown cheques and tried to steer him clear of the gang… but it was no use, he was too easy'[18].

It wasn't just the publican who had trouble with the travellers, however. One story of their time at the billabong, suggests that Jimmy Woodford recognised a horse that had been stolen from him, and he was intending to repossess it, until the new 'owner,' a renowned smuggler from Borroloola named 'Māori Jack' Reid[19], refused to give it up.

However, Woodford insisted, and to stop him taking it, Reid shot and killed the poor horse. The gang, all of them horsemen, took offence. They 'arrested' Reid and hung him upside down from a tree beside the billabong. This action fits with what we know of the men – all of them thought too highly of horses to allow such cruelty to go unpunished. It also gives a reason for Māori Jack's brother-in-law, Jim Carmody, to leave his kin behind, join the twelve, and make it a group of thirteen.

There was a fresh beast hanging from a frame in the meat house ready to butcher. Drunk, the men offered to buy some of it, but for reasons that can only be guessed at, they were refused. Maybe it had already been sold, and Bowen and Kirwin were planning to butcher it the next day. Or maybe they were sick of the obnoxious behaviour of a group of drunken overlanders, who were unable to pay their bill. Kirwin sent them packing.

They took the beef anyway, and dined well on steak that night, in their Bitter Springs camp.

Kirwin was no coward. The next morning, he stormed downed to their camp, harangued them, challenged them for payment, and then to fight for it. Some of the group had already been together for weeks, so they knew their best fighter to be the Scotsman, Hughie Campbell. Fists flew furiously, and Kirwin was weakened by a recent bout of malaria, and he was soon defeated - with his arm broken. Campbell's victory, thought the gang, gave them rights to the beef. Ernestine Hill explained it simply:

> … "your best man to our best man, and if we lose, we pay."
> Such was the law in the Territory then, and for a long time
> after[20].

Gaunt's version of the fight is a little different:

> … The fight was a short one, Kirwin having the best of it, but
> he could not last, Campbell's brute strength telling on him.
> Kirwin had just about got over a heavy dose of fever, in fact
> had it on him at the time. Had he been in trim, he would have
> whipped any one man in the bunch. He [Kirwin] … became
> weak and exhausted and "threw up the sponge." So much for
> the fight[21].

This first foray into crime together – thieving and the passing of worthless cheques – forged the thirteen travellers into a gang. To compound their crime, before they left they:

> … broke in the back of his store and stole about 3 cwt. of
> horseshoes[22], nails, flour, sugar, and sundry other articles, and
> we [Gaunt] and the other campers had no beef for breakfast
> that morning[23].

Thirteen armed men, travelling by horseback along the stock routes of the Northern Territory, with the nearest police hundreds of miles away, were a formidable force. A gang, of course, needs a name. Charles Gaunt wrote an explanation how they got theirs:

> Steve Lacey… christened them the "Ragged Thirteen". He
> asked Jack Daly [sic], one of the gang, "who was that little
> ragged fellow who was camped at the Springs?"
> "What little fellow?" asked Daly.

"That fellow that is camped with the big mob," replied Lacy.

"Oh," said Daly, "that fellow is one of us thirteen," and from those few words the "Ragged Thirteen" was born[24].

On the face of it, this is as good a reason as any, and if Gaunt actually rode with them for a while, he might have remembered correctly. But others tell different tales:

One suggests that the boss-drover, Nat Buchanan, had seen the South Australian contingent camped at Johnstons Waterhole[25], and called them a 'ragged bunch', and the name stuck. Or, as Hill suggested, it was aided by a comment made by storekeeper, Thomas Cashman[26]:

> … It was "Bluey" Buchanan, the grand old pioneer of Wave Hill, who camped with them at Frew's Ponds, tallied them up and told them they were the devil's number. It was a cattleman named Cashman, looking for them with wrath in his eye, near the "Blind Tiger" sly grog at Katherine, who gave them their name. When asked which 13 he was looking for, the only name Cashman could remember was Tommy the Rag and so the devil's dozen became the Ragged Thirteen[27].

Westward Ho

Whether they ever called themselves 'Ragged Thirteen' or not, the gang needed to follow the overlander's road to the west that departed from 'The Katherine'[28]. So, with full tucker bags and new horseshoes[29] that were 'worth a king's ransom', according to Ernestine Hill, that is where they headed. Katherine, then called Emungalan, was a small town gathered along the southern bank of the Katherine River, near the Telegraph Station. Clearly, its main reason for existence was the telegraph, but other locations in Emungalan included Bernard (Barney) Murphy's Cash Store, a butcher, a racetrack, several camps used by overlanders, cattlemen and miners, and the Blind Tiger sly-grog shop. Barney Murphy applied for a publican's licence in December 1886 and opened the Sportsman Hotel soon after[30].

Small though the town was, it was certainly large enough for overlanders to find newspapers and stay connected with the news of the world. In 1886, there were two local newspapers printed in Palmerston. They were the *Northern Territory Times and Gazette* and the *North Australian*. Each was a 4-page broadsheet which competed for advertisers, and to retain the *Government Gazette* contract. The front and back pages were kept for classified advertisements, but the rest was filled with editorials, letters to the editor, court reports, council news, telegraphed news, sports news, and shipping intelligence. As a plus, there was often room for original poetry or a funny story. A section of the *North Australian*, called 'Things and Others' and a similar section in the *Times* called 'News and Notes,' usually contained information about the goings-on in the bush – who was where, movement of cattle, or information on the opening of shops or hotels, and the like. On 28 May 1886, there was encouraging news about the Kimberley gold rush in 'Things and Others':

> The excitement respecting the Kimberley goldfields is being well kept up in the southern colonies. Large numbers are rushing to Derby from all quarters, and several boats are now on their way to the Sound, via Port Darwin. The steamer *Victoria* left Sydney for King's Sound on the 27th, intending to call in at Cambridge Gulf[31].

Everyone who could read in the bush would read the papers, when they could get them, no matter how old the news. Overlanders, like the Ragged Thirteen, read them repeatedly, and the *North Australian* of 11 June would certainly have raised their excitement – everything was saying "hurry to the Kimberley". On page 3, under the heading *The Kimberley Goldfields*[32], was a report from Tom Kilfoyle, with essential information for the travellers:

> Goldfields are situated on the Elvire River, which runs into the Panton River, and the Panton runs into the Ord eight miles above Osmand and Panton's cattle station. The total distance from the cattle station to the diggings is about eighty-five miles. A good track all the way.
>
> Diggers are supplied with abundance of meat from the above station.

Latest reports brought down by Mr. O'Donnell, the late explorer – who is now packing rations from Cambridge Gulf to the diggings – is that every man who was first on the field has got gold, most of them in good quantities. A lot of gold is being held on the field.

Billy Carpenter had 60 oz.; Hedley's party a good quantity; and Jack Horrigan about 100 oz. Everyone who has been down for rations has had gold. McPhee and Leonard Elvey took down about 70 oz. to Cambridge Gulf last trip, fine rough coarse gold. One piece weighed 4 oz.

Value of gold on the field is £3 15s. per oz. At Cambridge Gulf, it brings £4 per oz. Its actual value is about £4 2s. 6d. per oz.

Mr. O'Donnell sold one load of rations on the diggings at the following rates: Flour, 1s. 3d. per lb.; sugar, 1s.; tea, 4s. per lb.

Distance of goldfield from Cambridge Gulf by a new track to be opened by Mr. O'Donnell will be about 170 miles. Mr. Kilfoyle recommend that people going to diggings by sea should get out at Cambridge Gulf and also bring horses with them. If travelling by land from the Katherine the distance would be about 580 miles and a good road. The furthest stage without water is twenty miles.

When Mr. O'Donnell came down to Cambridge Gulf there were about 70 men working and all had gold. The country at diggings getting dry.

Mr Price, Government Resident at Cambridge Gulf, is going to visit the goldfield for the purpose of proclaiming it a goldfield. No wardens there yet, and no Chinese allowed. The sinking is only ten inches. No gold has been discovered on the Margaret. Mr. Kilfoyle returns from the Katherine to Kimberley on Friday and will take a mail. A great number of Queensland diggers are passing the Katherine every week on their way to the Kimberley goldfields[33].

Everyone in the fields, it seems, was having success. Encouraged, all the Thirteen had to do was to get there.

West Australian Surveyor General John Forrest detailed the route through the Territory, proudly announcing that it followed his brother's 1879 exploration route:

The route from Port Darwin would no doubt be up the telegraph line to the Katherine station, a distance of 170 miles, thence to the Victoria River, up the Wickham, and to the junction of the Negri River with the Ord, and thence up the Ord to the goldfield; in fact, from the Katherine telegraph station to the goldfields would be along the route of my brother in 1879, and the distance is 400 miles from the Katherine, or from Port Darwin 570 miles to where the bulk of the gold has been found[34].

But getting to Western Australia wasn't as easy as it sounded. The distance was huge, and the tracks passed through country where local Indigenous people were using armed resistance tactics against the white invaders:

News of another native outrage comes to us from the Victoria River. Mr. Lindsay Crawford, manager of Messrs. Fisher and Lyons' Victoria River Station, telegraphed to Mr. H. W. H. Stevens, under date of April 21st, that William Jackson, a bullock driver, employed on the road to Fisherton depot, had been speared by the blacks. The wound, which is in the man's neck, is not considered dangerous, or likely to prove fatal[35].

The local tribes had the advantage of an intimate knowledge of their lands, and they knew the track between the waterholes that every overlander would travel. After a guerilla style attack, most could withdraw into the rugged escarpment areas, where white men on horseback could not go:

The track generally used is lined with pinnacle hills, which shelter the natives and admit them committing outrages unseen by the victims[36].

Their major disadvantage was their technology: spears and woomeras versus modern repeating rifles, and this was to be a deciding factor in their eventual fate. Another was the willingness of some white men to 'disperse' the tribes with lead and burn the bodies of the fallen – men like Jack Watson and Lindsay Crawford had many dozens of victims on their ledgers.

Aboriginal resistance was ongoing. In September 1886:

A telegram received in Palmerston during the week states

Figure 12: 'Dispersal' of Aborigines by Native Police (Queensland) by Carl Lumholtz, 1889.

that still another outrage is to be added to the long list of such affairs perpetrated by the Northern Territory blacks. Three men, named Hibbert, Williams, and Matthew Cahill, employed as stockmen on the Victoria River Station, were camped on the Little Gregory Creek, about two miles from the Gregory, between the Victoria and Delamere Stations, the former being distant some 100 miles and the latter about 35 miles.

Williams and Cahill went fishing, leaving Hibbert in camp. Whilst engaged fishing, they were suddenly attacked by the natives. Williams was killed instantly. One of the spears struck Cahill in the upper part of the back and passed downwards and out on the opposite side of the body, cutting a very ugly flesh wound all along. He succeeded in effecting his escape by a miracle[37].

Williams, who was speared through the neck, became the first white man to be killed on the Victoria River frontier.

The *North Australian* editor, reporting the tragedy, helped ensure his readers' fear and loathing of the tribes remained high:

The part of the country in which this outrage occurred is said to be *infested by savage tribes of natives*, and travellers who have been there state that extreme caution should be exercised when passing through[38] [emphasis added].

It is unlikely that the Ragged Thirteen avoided meeting or seeing Aboriginal people, but they also may not have 'needed' to employ any violent strategies against the tribes as they passed across their lands. Thirteen armed men travelling together were a formidable group, and there is no evidence that anyone attacked them as they moved west, but no one would have been surprised[39].

If the Thirteen did have to defend themselves, atrocities may indeed have occurred as a result, because it was a time when white men killing 'myall blacks' was common. The Thirteen would have heard about it, and known some of the worst perpetrators, and also they would have known how rare it was for a white man to be brought to justice for any crimes against Aboriginal people. If they themselves were ever involved, they kept very quiet about it. Nevertheless, according to Thomas Nugent's great-grandson, Billy Fitz, his family believes Nugent to have been a 'bad man... who shot Aboriginals... shot anyone who got in his way,' and that he was a 'cohort of Ned Kelly'[40].

No records were ever kept, but in 1933, *The Sunday Sun* newspaper in Sydney was not convinced that they were merely 'larrikins of the bush', as many writers have portrayed them. As the Thirteen crossed the Territory to Western Australia, said the paper:

> ... death stared them in the face a score of times and the
> hostility of the blacks became more marked as the party drew
> near the West Australian border. Skirmishes occurred, but
> details of what actually happened have died with the Thirteen.
> Perhaps skeletons out in the desert sands tell a mute story of
> eventualities fifty years ago[41].

The Thirteen were now under the leadership of Tom Nugent, who was calling himself Tom Holmes. Fully informed, by the newspapers and the 'bush telegraph', of the difficulties travellers might face on the 930 km (580 miles) road to Halls Creek, he ensured the Thirteen functioned as a protective group. Watches were necessary at night when they camped, in the same way many of the men were used to when droving, and horses needed to be cared for, hobbled each night, and tailed early in the morning.

Everything the travellers needed, such as tobacco, flour, tea, and sugar, spare horseshoes, tools and camping equipment, was carried by packhorses.

Being happy to duff the cattle they needed, branded or not, the Ragged Thirteen never went short of meat. Butcher 'New England' Jack Woods could cut up a beast as quickly as the best of them, and they would then jerk beef for consumption on the road and cut greenhide strips from the hides to replace worn spancels, bridles, stock whips or anything else they needed. They had enough to share their bounty with other travellers and struggling station workers, and their hospitality became famous.

But stores run out. Flour and sugar are eaten, tobacco smoked, and the tea drunk. Also, horseshoes and riding equipment wear out. The Thirteen had thirty or forty horses between them, and these needed to be shod and cared for properly. The horseshoes they had stolen at Abraham's Billabong were used up as they crossed large swathes of stony country, and other rations were also consumed. But any problems this might have caused were easily solved when they arrived at Victoria River Downs Station (VRD).

Victoria River Downs

There were two main routes to Victoria River Downs Station from Katherine – as there are today. The first joined a new stock route that had been opened a few months before by Nat Buchanan and Sam Croker. It was formally called the Murranji Stock Route in 1886, but it was always difficult country. Few rivers cross it, water is unreliable, and lancewood and bulwaddy thickets abound. There are also areas of 'drummy' ground that vibrate under a herd, and this can spook the cattle. Buchanan's track left the telegraph line near Newcastle Waters and travelled northwest. Today it is crossed by the Buchanan Highway, which started as a 'beef road' in 1966. It leaves the Stuart Highway near Dunmarra and crosses to Top Springs, where it meets at a crossroads with the Buntine Highway. The Buntine travels south from the more northern Victoria Highway, and then goes all the way to the Western Australian border.

The Thirteen's most likely route was on the trail that headed southwest from Katherine, via Delamere Station, to somewhere near where Top Springs is now, on a branch of the Victoria River. From there they may have either travelled southwest, to Wave Hill, or made a more direct route, straight to the Western Australian border, near Nicholson Station.

The dirt road constructed from Timber Creek to Top Springs, via Victoria River Downs, was known as the 'Victoria River Downs Road'. It passes through Jasper Gorge, and it is now called the Buchanan Highway all the way, extending the section that arrives at

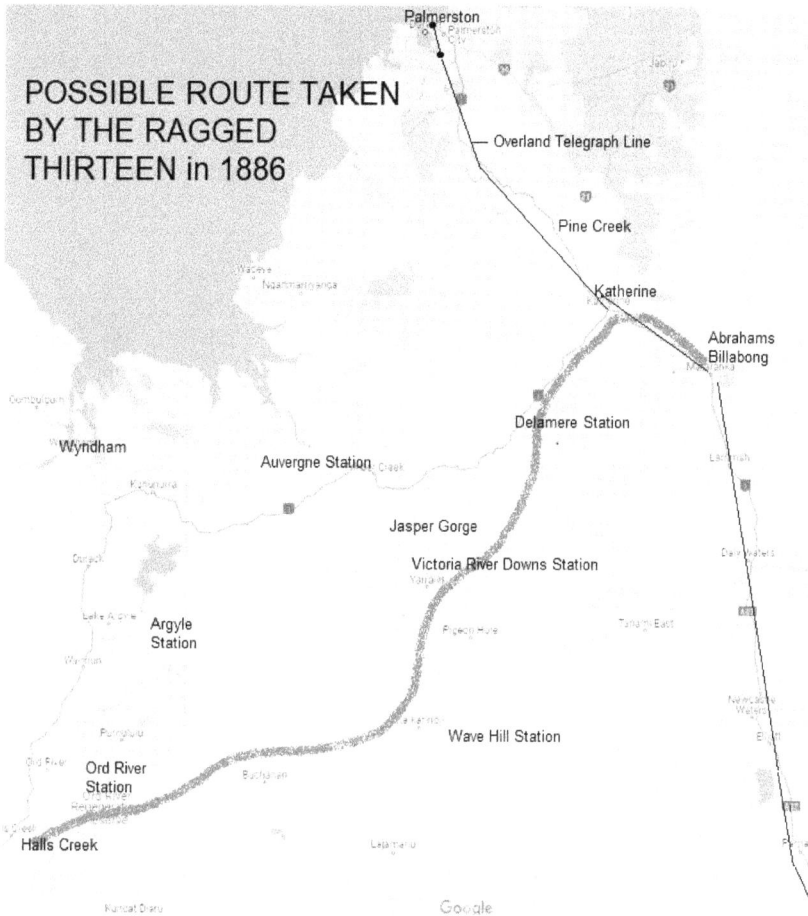

POSSIBLE ROUTE TAKEN
BY THE RAGGED
THIRTEEN in 1886

Palmerston

Overland Telegraph Line

Pine Creek

Katherine

Abrahams
Billabong

Delamere Station

Wyndham

Auvergne Station

Jasper Gorge

Victoria River Downs Station

Argyle
Station

Wave Hill Station

Ord River
Station

Halls Creek

Google

Map 2: A possible route taken by the Ragged Thirteen from Abraham's Billabong to Halls Creek.

Top Springs from the Stuart Highway.

From Katherine, Timber Creek and Western Australia are now reached more directly via the Victoria Highway. This highway developed from a series of tracks that formed between the cattle stations. It remained unsealed until the 1950s.

Apart from realignments around swampy areas, or other difficult terrains, all overlanders in the late 1880s took one of these tracks. Hundreds of miners, like the Ragged Thirteen, heading to Halls Creek, mostly used the track that crossed the plains to the east of Victoria River Downs. This country belonged to a tribe of people called the

Figure 13: VRD Head Station on the Wickham River in 1891 (SLSA B-10127).

Karangpurru. They were 'people of the plains' who had no rough escarpment country to retire to and shelter in like their neighbours in times of conflict. Contact with the miners and cattlemen often meant one thing. As Darrell Lewis explains, their population was decimated in a few years[42].

> ... during 1886 the track was used by hundreds of miners heading for the Kimberley goldfield. Many of the overlanding miners were of very bad character- 'the scum of the back blocks' -and extremely brutal towards Aborigines. Justice Charles Dashwood, the Government Resident between 1892 and 1905, spoke to a number of the early Northern Territory pioneers, including Jack Watson and the famous buffalo hunter, Paddy Cahill. The stories they told Dashwood about events along the overland track to the Kimberley led him to claim that the Aborigines along the route had been 'shot like crows'[43].

VRD was a large station by any standards. It was, and for decades would remain, the largest cattle station in the world. In 1886, the homestead was little more than a rough and ready series of sheds and corrugated iron huts. The huts housed the manager, Lindsay Crawford, the cattlemen, cook, and other station workers. Lindsay had established the station just three years earlier and, like other stations in the area, certainly saw benefit in the ready market the Halls Creek gold rush offered him. But the rush also brought problems. Goldsbrough and Mort, who took over ownership of the station from Fisher and Lyons, after they experienced financial difficulties, regularly sent their agent, Hildebrand Stevens, to monitor the success of the venture. In a report from July 1887, Stevens wrote that:

> Mr. Crawford has also had to exercise the greatest caution to prevent the hundreds of overlanders, who have passed through to Kimberley from making away with the Station horses & killing the cattle for beef. A muster of the horses in April showed no losses. Where men have passed without money beef only has been supplied to them to prevent them helping themselves[44].

Caution wasn't always enough. Four years later, in October 1891, Stevens reported that:

> … Thefts committed by gangs of horse stealers passing thro' the country en route to Kimberley and W. Aust. have, on some runs, been enormous. Mr J.A. Macartney, our neighbour on the Victoria, has lost over 100 head in this manner[45].

When the Thirteen arrived in late 1886, Crawford and most of his employees were away with the cattle, and in charge of the homestead was a 'new chum' bookkeeper, named Ted Lockett (or Lockhart).

Tom Nugent knew much about the running of cattle stations. He had worked in many, and even set one up from scratch, so he no doubt knew the layout of the place without ever seeing it. As the Thirteen approached the homestead, he hatched a plan.

The gang pulled up and camped far enough away for their presence to remain unknown. Then Nugent, dressing as smartly as he could, approached the homestead and hailed poor Lockett. Explaining that he was a well-to-do squatter, looking to start his own station somewhere and looking for land, he accepted Lockett's invitation to a drink, a meal, and a place to sleep. Then the two of them sat on the veranda with their first bottle of rum and played cards. A garrulous man, Nugent had no trouble in entertaining the storeman, and repeatedly filled his cup. Soon Lockett was very drunk indeed[46].

In the meantime, the rest of the gang crept quietly to the back of the station store. Removing some of the wall, they then had unfettered access to as much food and equipment as they could carry. And it was a lot. Their prize included five-hundred-weight of new horseshoes (250kg, or about 210 horseshoes), tobacco, tea, boots, treacle, flour, and whatever else was available.

As already mentioned, the Halls Creek gold rush provided a ready market for VRD cattle. The station was only three years old, but the fine pastures and flat land to its west meant that cattle could easily be taken across to the Halls Creek stockyards. It was sold there to a butcher named Peter Fox. Lindsay Crawford himself used the stock route to take two hundred head of cattle to Halls Creek in 1886[47]; perhaps this was where he was when the Ragged Thirteen raided his station.

In Halls Creek, the miners paid for their meat with gold, and consequently, so did Peter Fox. Crawford kept this in a tin under his kitchen table. Had the Ragged Thirteen been aware that a box of nuggets, worth more than £1000, was within such easy reach, they would have struck it rich[48], and their history would be very different. A thousand pounds in 1886, is equivalent to about $300,000 today.

Nevertheless, they had a huge haul – the largest heist the Thirteen are known to have pulled. It is the event that most qualifies them to be called bushrangers. They knew that their thieving would gain attention, so they packed up and quickly headed west for the Negri River, and the border that was less than 300 km away. If any police found their trail, Nugent knew they would not follow them into Western Australia.

The route that the Thirteen took to the border, and from there to Halls Creek, was easy to follow. Huge herds had blazed the trail when the Duracks and MacDonalds had brought their cattle over from Queensland, and many smaller herds had used it since – including Crawford's two hundred. For skilled bushmen like the Thirteen, following the tracks must have been like following a six-lane freeway. Others were on the trail too. In 1942, an old man named C.L. Goodby, recalled meeting them on the road. He wrote to the *Western Mail*:

> … It was in November or December 1886, when they were on their way to Halls Creek at the time of the Kimberley rush, that I met them between Victoria Downs station and the Ord River. None of them wore shirts and I think they were the first to introduce the non-wearing of shirts among the Europeans. I did not know any of them personally. They were very much talked about among those who overlanded to Halls Creek in 1886 and 1887. It is a long time ago and a lot of the old hands have gone west since then, but still I feel sure that there are a good few left and no doubt you will receive news from some of them. "The Ragged 13" were a good lot of rough bushmen, and from what I knew of them, they were well liked[49].

The Thirteen travelled quickly and arrived in Western Australia, unmolested, towards the end of 1886, or early in 1887. Unaware that they were at the tail-end of a rush that was about to peter out, they were ready to dig up their fortunes in the goldfields of Halls Creek.

A short postscript of the gang's raid on VRD comes from Donald Swan's reminiscences. A man named Ashton, who might have been a guest at the station, was in the wrong place at the wrong time. He carried a reputation forward:

> … a broken-down Queensland squatter, known as the "Tea and Tobacco Bushranger," owing to a slight misunderstanding on his way overland at the Victoria River Downs Station. On his arrival at the homestead, he found the "Ragged Thirteen" in possession, they having got the storekeeper, Ted Lockett, a popular and likeable fellow, very badly drunk. The Unlucky Number ran through the store, stealing a 22lb. case of tobacco and a small chest of tea, for which theft poor old Ashton got the blame[50].

Endnotes

1 *Livistona rigida.*
2 *North Australian*, 19 December 1884, page 3.
3 Robert (Bob) C.S. McPhee went on to seek out shorter routes for cattle droves towards Western Australia, rather than via Katherine. He then joined the gold rush to Halls Creek with Augustus Lucanus. He appears regularly in various reminiscences published in *Kimberley Scenes* (Clement and Bridge).
4 *Northern Territory Times and Gazette*, 16 May 1885, page 3.
5 *North Australian*, 17 September 1886, page 2.
6 Mat Kirwin had lived in the goldfields in the Port Darwin Camp and Grove Hill for several years, and his name appears on various racing club notices of the early 1880s.
7 *Northern Territory Times and Gazette*, 20 September 1884, page 1.
8 *Northern Territory Times and Gazette*, 11 June 1887, page 2, page 3, and 13 September 1884, page 3.
9 *North Australian*, 30 Jul 1886, Page 2, Things And Others. M.D. Armstrong was a butcher, import/export businessman and cattleman with wide business interests. He was killed in Palmerston by the 1897 cyclone. Adam Bryden was the Manager of the Commercial Bank in Palmerston, and part-owner of the Roper Bar Hotel, and the store at Abraham's Billabong between 1884 and 1886.
10 David Lindsay, *Adelaide Observer*, 18 August 1888, page 42: The Traveller, Port Darwin to the Ruby Fields.
11 *North Australian*, 19 December 1884, page 3, Notes From The Overland Track Between Katherine And Queensland.
12 *North Australian*, 29 May 1885, page 2, Things And Others.
13 *Northern Territory Times and Gazette*, 28 August 1886, page 3.
14 *North Australian*, 24 September 1886, page 2, Things And Others.
15 *North Australian*, 17 September 1886, page 2.
16 *Northern Standard*, 18 September 1931, page 4.
17 Charles Gaunt, *Northern Standard*, 18 September 1931, page 4: Old Time Memories.
18 Charles Gaunt, *Northern Standard*, 18 September 1931, page 4: Old Time Memories.
19 Māori Jack Reid later lived for many years next door to Charles Gaunt in Pine Creek. In Borroloola, he was the skipper of the *Good Intent*, bringing in stores from Burketown. He was a renowned smuggler of rum.
20 Ernestine Hill (1951).
21 Charles Gaunt, *Northern Standard*, 18 September 1931, page 4: Old Time Memories.
22 3 hundred weight is about 150 kilograms, or about the weight of 135 standard sized horseshoes.
23 Charles Gaunt, *Northern Standard*, 18 September 1931, page 4: Old Time Memories.

24 Charles Gaunt, *Northern Standard*, 18 September 1931, page 4: Old Time Memories.

25 There is a Johnstons Waterhole near Dunmarra and a Johnstons Waterhole on Delamere Station. Both were used by the gang, but it is likely that Buchanan was at the former with them. Alan Giles described it in 1875: "The usual halting-places on the journey are McGorrorey's Pond, 14 miles on Auld's Pond, three miles further Milner's Lagoon, another 14 miles then Johnston's Lagoon (12 miles distant), and next on eight miles to Frew's Pond. (Allan Giles, *Adelaide Observer*, 18 December 1875, page 11, Central Australian Notes.).

26 Thomas Cashman was issued a licence to keep a store at Cresswell Creek, near the Powell's Creek Telegraph Station. (*Northern Territory Times and Gazette*, 5 December 1885, page 2), so maybe Abraham's Billabong was not their first crime: Cashman appears in various versions of the story as being 'after' them. He may have been robbed at Cresswell Creek before they reached Abraham's Billabong. (Cashman was also a drover in the McArthur River area, *Northern Territory Times and Gazette*, 12 September 1885).

27 Ernestine Hill (1951).

28 The Murranji Track from Newcastle Waters was opened in 1886, saving many hundreds of kilometres of droving (G. Buchanan, *Packhorse and Waterhole*, 1933, p. 121).

29 Spare horseshoes were essential, as O'Donnell's journal shows during his exploration to the Kimberley: "After this we got into very rough limestone country, on the whole of which were strewed broken and sharp pointed slabs of that stone. The consequence was that several of the horses had their shoes torn off and their feet cut about in a terrible manner" (*The Argus*, 12 January 1884).

30 *Northern Territory Times and Gazette*, 18 December 1886.

31 *North Australian*, 28 May 1886, page 2, Things And Others.

32 *North Australian*, 11 June 1886, Page 3, The Kimberley Goldfields.

33 *North Australian*, 11 June 1886, Page 3, The Kimberley Goldfields.

34 *Brisbane Courier*, 9 July 1886, page 3, The Kimberley District.

35 *Northern Territory Times and Gazette*, 1 May 1886, page 2: New and Notes.

36 *North Australian*. 17 September 1886, page 2: *Another Outrage by Blacks*.

37 *North Australian*. 17 September 1886, page 2: *Another Outrage by Blacks*.

38 *North Australian*. 17 September 1886, page 2: *Another Outrage by Blacks*.

39 This doesn't mean it didn't happen – 'punishing' Aboriginal tribes was so common in the bush it must have seemed like normal behaviour. Many events must have happened that were never mentioned by any of the protagonists.

40 Comment by the late Billy Fitz, Nugent's great grandson, in an oral interview with Kylie Stevenson, 2020. Fitz was also the great grandson of Billy Miller Linklater, whom he called his 'Scottish grandfather', whereas Nugent was his 'Irish grandfather'.

41 *The Sunday Sun* (Sydney), 12 February 1933, p 3.

42 Many Karangpurru people today call the community of Yarralin, N.T., their home.

43 Lewis, 2004.

44 Stevens, 11 July 1887, in Lewis 2021.
45 Stevens, 9 October 1891, in Lewis 2021.
46 Edward Lockett was no innocent lamb either. Listed in Darryl Lewis's *Victoria River District Doomsday Book* as the storekeeper in 1885 or 1886, and stockman in May 1887, by 1889 he was wanted for embezzlement. Police described him as 'a stout man about 27 years old, about 5 ft 7 in. Dark Brown Hair, scanty, Dark Eyes, Sallow Complexion, Scar on right hip from recent Spear wound'. He was last recorded as going to the 'Pilbara Goldfields', and the police were after him there (Lewis, 2021).
47 *Northern Territory Times and Gazette*, 16 October 1886, page 3.
48 Stevens, 1887.
49 Western Mail (Perth), 12 March 1942, page 38.
50 Donald Swan ('A. Pioneer'), *Western Mail* (Perth), 5 September 1929, page 9: *Kimberley Scenes*.

Chapter 3
Western Australia

The Kimberley

In 1879, Alexander Forrest led the first exploration party through the Kimberley. He was an experienced explorer and had accompanied his brother John Forrest across Western Australia, from Perth to Adelaide, in 1870, and again, from Geraldton to the Overland Telegraph Line near The Peake, in South Australia, in 1874.

Eventually, both brothers played a large part in the Kimberley's conquest. John's interest came through his position of surveyor-general from 1883, when he established the towns of Derby and Wyndham, and later as Western Australia's first premier, from 1890.

Alexander Forrest's 1879 journey, across the Kimberley to the Northern Territory, nearly ended in disaster when they ran out of supplies. But he famously saved his team by leaving them to rest beside a waterhole, going ahead the last 160 km to the Overland Telegraph Line to get help, and then returning to collect them.

There was great interest in his arrival in the Territory, and in what he had seen in the west. In Pine Creek, surrounded by gold miners who were a part of the Territory's own gold rush, he described a country that was similar to that they were already mining. Could it be auriferous? Some thought it worth checking out. Two high-profile prospectors and owners of the largest holdings on the Territory goldfields, Phil Saunders and Adam Johns, hired a schooner named *Prospect* at Port Darwin. They then shipped horses and packs to Cossack, in Western

Australia, to follow Forrest's trail to the East Kimberley in 1881. Theirs was a self-funded journey lasting 14 months, and they searched the country thoroughly. Unfortunately, the only 'colour' they found was near the headwaters of the Ord River[1], and when Adam Johns became ill, temporarily losing his sight, and suffering from problems with his spleen, they returned home to the Territory. Their report listed what they had found, and they optimistically applied for the reward offered by the Western Australian Government for finding the first payable goldfield in the colony. They were ignored.

In 1883, the Kimberley was once again in the news, when William J. (Billy) O'Donnell and William Carr-Boyd were sent, by a private syndicate of investors known as the Cambridge Downs Pastoral Association[2], to look for land upon which they could build a sheep station.

O'Donnell was a member of the Victorian Exploring Party that had brought back the remains of Burke and Wills in 1864. Twenty years later, having mastered his profession of explorer, O'Donnell left Palmerston and travelled through to the Kimberley via the Territory's Victoria River Region, to examine the land.

Carr-Boyd was also an experienced explorer, and although not the expedition leader, his name quickly became more well known. In fact, many of the newspapers of the time called O'Donnell's expedition the *Carr-Boyd Expedition*. This would have pleased him, but because he had already been second-in-command to William Hodgkinson, exploring the Diamantina River area of Queensland in 1875, he was miffed, and jealous, that he had been overlooked for the leadership in this new exploration.

Carr-Boyd was originally a cattleman – working as a jackeroo, from the age of nine, in the Barcoo region of Queensland for over a decade. Somewhere along the line, he developed excellent writing skills, and was soon corresponding to Queensland newspapers under the name of 'Potjostler'. He was also interested in prospecting, and worked at least one season on the Palmer River goldfields, inland from Cairns.

In 1880, then 28-years-old, Carr-Boyd had mounted a private expedition to search for his brothers, Cornelius ('Syd') and Albert Prout, who had disappeared on the Barkly Tableland when looking for new country. Carr-Boyd found their dehydrated corpses beside their camp, where they had died of thirst, two years previously.

Determined to leave Queensland in 1883, Carr-Boyd originally planned to head to Victoria, but instead agreed to fill a position in O'Donnell's Expedition.

The party of seven left Katherine on 26 March 1883, with twenty-six horses and provisions for six months. Apart from William Carr-Boyd, there were Surveyor A. W. Wells, John O'Malley, David Linacre, and O'Donnell's brother-in-law, Henry Wall.

An Aboriginal man of the Wardaman tribe, who was never named in the records, was recruited by Carr-Boyd from Delamere Station to work as his 'boy'.

Months passed, and by September some in the cities were getting worried, because no one had heard anything from the expedition. There were calls to get them help:

> The Government has been asked to assist in discovering the fate of the expedition which left Queensland five months ago under the leadership of Mr. Carr-Boyd for Kimberley, and which is supposed to have been lost or killed by the blacks. The Colonial Secretary says that the Government has no means at present of communicating with the survey parties at Kimberley[3].

But their worry was unnecessary, said one of Carr-Boyd's friends.

> Eight hundred miles of country to travel; say, to make even a superficial examination twelve miles a day or sixty-six days; forming the station a month, little enough even to mark the boundaries of a property 3125 miles in area; then prospecting for gold, which is an alluring pursuit of indefinite duration, and finally return out via Roebuck Bay and Perth. Mr. Boyd has now been out six months, far too brief a time to create anxiety for his safety, and if I can inspire the same confidence

in his relatives and friends as I feel myself, they will dismiss what I trust are premature fears[4].

Carr-Boyd had told this friend that he intended prospecting for gold. He was mindful of the Western Australian Government's offer of a £5000 reward for a payable goldfield. "I think we have a good chance of finding one," he wrote to his friend. "I think I shall go in by Roebuck Bay[5], and round by Perth and Adelaide".

John O'Malley later said that Carr-Boyd told the manager of the Katherine Telegraph Station, before they left, that he was not returning to Katherine. He was planning to go to Perth instead[6].

Carr-Boyd made several side-trips from O'Donnell's party to fossick for gold, while O'Donnell remained focussed on finding land for the sheep station. Then, as he had suggested he would, he resigned from the expedition on 10 August. Despite O'Donnell's protestations, he took his share of the rations, and his Aboriginal assistant, and headed off towards Roebuck Bay.

Ten days later he was back, very weak, suffering from both dysentery and scurvy. His rations had begun to run out, so he had wisely returned to the expedition.

O'Donnell ensured that the rest of his expedition was professionally managed and, after eight months in the bush, the men were "in as good health and spirits as when last at Palmerston". When they finally returned to the Overland Telegraph Line in October, O'Donnell wrote to the *Times* by telegraph from Katherine:

> … I am sorry that I cannot send you full particulars of trip through Western Australia. Must give first report to Syndicate in whose interest we were sent out, but will give you brief outline of travels through your Territory. Making a final start from Dr Browne's cattle station, Delamere, and steering on a general South by West course, and parallel to the Victoria, we reached the latter river in 125 miles. After running the Victoria up for three days we struck a large tributary, which we followed for 20 miles. This creek I have called Giles Creek, after Mr A. Giles, of Springvale, who was very kind to us. After running up Giles Creek for one day we crossed over and

came on some splendidly grassed downs and plains, until we struck the course of another large tributary of the Victoria...[7]

When his 20,000-word report on the Kimberley was finally published, it drew the interest of more than the Cambridge Downs Pastoral Association:

> ... I have, beyond doubt, proved that a vast area of
> magnificent pastoral lands exists in the hitherto unexplored
> portions of the Kimberley district, and as I have had
> considerable experience in Queensland, I can safely say that
> these lands will compare favourably with the best parts of
> that colony. It is suitable for any description of stock, horses,
> cattle, or sheep. I have never seen anything to approach it with
> regard to its waters, as we daily met with several watercourses,
> many of large size, and nearly all contained running springs,
> the whole of the country being made available thereby. With
> respect to the timber, I found it most suitable for all purposes,
> and everywhere plentiful. I made it my particular duty to look
> carefully for the presence of poison plants but failed to find
> any. I also noticed that there were no injurious grass seeds.
> The animals which inhabit this country are not numerous,
> being chiefly kangaroos, and very few wallaby. Native dogs
> are also very scarce, as we saw and heard very few during the
> trip. Owing to these facts, combined with the delightfully
> cool climate which we enjoyed, I am convinced that before
> long this will become a great wool growing district. From the
> telegraph line (Northern Territory), we have proved that a
> good stock route can be made to the Ord River. The natives
> with whom we came in contact proved perfectly harmless.
> They will, no doubt, become very useful to future settlers.[8]

But all had not been well among the expeditioners. Carr-Boyd's personal side trips and then his decision to leave for Roebuck Bay caused much angst and he was resented for his not accepting a share of cooking and horse-tailing duties[9]. O'Donnell's report, tellingly co-signed by Surveyor Wells, concluded with thanks for *nearly* everyone:

> ... Before concluding I must return my sincere thanks to the
> members of my party for the support they gave me on every
> occasion. Although suffering great privations during portions
> of the trip, they all, with one exception, did their level best

to carry out my instructions, and to assist in bringing the expedition to a successful issue[10].

It was obvious who the 'one exception' was, and Carr-Boyd was furious. He responded immediately:

> ... Now, let me tell you Sir, that the above-named trip was conducted in the most disgraceful manner by O'Donnell from first to last, as my report to the Cambridge Downs Pastoral Association, when published, will show, which, in my vindication, I shall have to insist upon being published, which, I think, will take a good deal of the gloss and romance off the affair. I should be very sorry to let my friends think that I, being very considerably interested in the affair, could quietly look on and see the most glaring acts of misjudgement on the part of O'Donnell, without seriously remonstrating with him. Thank goodness, I have only to go to five or six of my own private exploring trips in the Northern Territory of South Australia and Queensland, with two public ones, which have been published, to show the public what I have done in that line. I hope, Sir, you will kindly insert this, as my name has been most unjustifiably dragged into print over this affair. – I am, &c.,
>
> W. J. H. CARR-BOYD[11].

Maintaining his rage, Carr-Boyd sued the Cambridge Downs Pastoral Association, specifically Secretary Arthur Davidson Cotton, for libel. The case was heard by Mr Justice Sir Edward Holroyd in the Supreme Court, Melbourne, on 28 May 1884, with Carr-Boyd claiming £5000 damages on account of a letter signed by Cotton and published in the *Argus*, accusing Carr-Boyd of desertion. His "endeavour to desert his comrades" wrote Cotton, "will condemn him with all men who know what pioneer work is"[12].

Justice Holroyd agreed with a full jury of twelve men, that there was no case of libel. Carr-Bord had wasted his money and their time.

In the meantime, the Western Australian Government recruited a geologist from the 'Irish Geological Survey,' named Edmund Hardmann to survey the Ord River region and look for gold. He found it too, in the same places that Saunders and Johns had discovered their 'colour'.

Hardmann's 1884 report led to Charles Hall, Jack Slattery, McCarthy, and others prospecting the area in 1885. They followed the report closely[13], and began prospecting along the creeks in the upper Ord region. Prospecting was easy in the wet season, when water trickled along the beds, but at first, they had to carry their dirt for two miles to available water. They found ten ounces (283 grams) in about 5 days. In September, the *Daily News* in Perth was happy to print Hall's report to the Government:

> The gold lay in the bed of the creek, quite close to the surface, merely covered by the drift sand[14].

There was no incentive to keep the find quiet. Hall and Slattery travelled to Perth and applied for the £5,000 reward. They then returned to the little creek in the bush and, on Christmas Day, 1885, Hall stumbled across the find of his life – a 28-ounce (793 gram) nugget! By May the next year, the news was well and truly out:

> The Government are in receipt of further intelligence from the Kimberley goldfields brought to Cossack, by the s. s. *Otway*, on her return from Derby. The Government Resident at Roebourne (Col. Angelo) wired yesterday that it was reported a further quantity of 250 ounces of gold was on board the *Otway*; that she had brought information confirmatory of the discovery of the 28-ounce nugget, and that Slattery [sic] was the finder of this nugget. Col. Angelo also mentions that various lots of gold — estimated at fully 2000 ounces — had reached Derby. Full official reports are coming by the *Otway*, which should reach Fremantle early next week[15].

Charles Hall travelled with the nugget and proudly showed it off to the press in Fremantle:

> … Mr. Charles Hall, who was the lucky finder of the 28 oz nugget at Kimberley arrived at Fremantle by the S.S *Otway* on Saturday morning and was interviewed by several persons anxious to have a peep at the nugget in question. It is an irregular oval in shape and the weight given its gross weight. Mr Hall has come to the metropolis to put in a claim for the £5000 bonus offered to the discoverer of a payable goldfield[16].

The nugget was sold to the government for display in the Colonial and Indian Exhibition. They paid Hall £10, but his real prize, if he could access it, was the £5000 reward that he was still hopeful of getting[17]. The nugget was exhibited in a shop window:

> It is now exhibited in Mr V. E. Nesbit's window in Hay
> Street… Its gross weight 28 oz 6 dwt. It is shown in the same
> state as when dug out of the mine, its edges are rough, the
> depressions still have some of the soil adhering to them, and
> the quartz can still be seen adhering to the gold. The length
> of the nugget is about 4 inches, its average width is about two
> and its thickness something over an inch[18].

Soon, *very soon*, after the announcement of the discovery in the Kimberley, the rush was on. Men joined it from all corners of the continent:

> Away in the far north of the continent, adventurous spirits
> have unearthed a few nuggets of gold. The news has spread far
> and wide, and in that glorious uncertainty that often sheds a
> charm over the road to death, hundreds have already gone to
> try their luck, and thousands are at this moment much in the
> humour to follow them. In one week, we have witnessed four
> large steamers leave Sydney for the north. Others have since
> taken their departure, and more are advertised to sail. Those
> that have gone already have sailed with a full complement of
> passengers[19].

The excitement was so great that words of caution were successfully ignored – like these from the *Daily Telegraph* in May 1886, written as the steam ship *Gambier* pulled away from the Sydney wharf, carrying 150 hopeful miners, and their sparkling new equipment:

> … it was apparent that beyond the horses, insufficient
> provision has been made to convey passengers on to the field.
> It is time more enterprise should be directed to trade, for
> we believe it will be found that the number going who are
> equipped as miners only is quite out of proportion to intended
> tradesmen. This, though usual, is to be regretted, inasmuch as
> prices of goods will not only be regulated by supply, but the
> field being so remote from centres of commerce, on altogether

insufficient supply may cause great hardship. There was a good quantity of stores of various kinds on board, but as for us, we could observe, the quantity was not in proportion to the number of persons who will be almost entirely dependent upon others to provide them with the necessities of life and with work[20].

But even the *Daily Telegraph* was excited. Their journalists interviewed some of the miners, and the 'camp-followers'. This latter group "were ready to do anything outside of digging, as long as they thought it paid better" and most had brought stores to sell or barter.

Two women were also on board:

> It was also somewhat surprising to see several of the weaker sex on board; but inquiry elicited that they had made money by trading on other goldfields, and it would not be for the want of determination if they did not make money at Kimberley[21].

These women were not 'weaker' at all. Mrs. McQuilty[22] and her maid, Miss Kitty Gannon, travelled to Wyndham to open a public house. On arrival in Wyndham, they set to work with such alacrity that the hotel and pub were open for business, according to Lucanus, just three weeks later[23].

It was a grand affair:

> … I think, by the way she is going about things, that the hotel that takes the preference to hers, will have to be something very good indeed; she has brought a piano with her, and has a large billiard table following, so it speaks very well for a commencement[24].

The piano brought Mrs. McQuilty a lot of business. Many writers mentioned it – and Mrs. McQuilty's marvellous voice.

William Carr-Boyd's arrival on the *Gambier* reconnected him with his old adversary, William O'Donnell. Clearly, they reconciled their differences and as the only men who had travelled through the Kimberley before, they were able to capitalise on their experiences. Lucanus recalled that together they "piloted the first lot of diggers to Hall's Creek at £1 per head"[25].

Of interest is the Aboriginal servant accompanying O'Donnell named Pompey. Lucanus wrote that Pompey had once been a part of the Aboriginal cricket team that travelled to England from Victoria in 1868, and he had even met the queen. Lucanus, a racist of the highest order, begrudged him some respect, writing that he was "rather civilised and sang a good song" and "he could box well"[26].

Covering most of the journey in the relative comfort of a steam ship was one thing, but crossing the entire continent by foot was another:

> A drover who lately came through from Queensland with a mob of horses, which he intended taking to Kimberley until the bad reports made him alter his course, says that he passed hundreds of men making for the Kimberley Goldfields, and even when they reach the Katherine and are supplied with the latest information concerning the field, they still express a determination to go on to the end of their journey. Fabulous prices have been offered to Mr. Murray [of the Katherine Telegraph Station] for provisions, flour in particular, but on account of having only a small supply at the station, travellers could not be accommodated to the full extent of their wishes.

> Regarding the mortality of Kimberley, a correspondent writes us from the Gulf: - "There are two things which will never be correctly cleared up viz.; the number of ounces of gold unearthed, and the number of men buried in Western Australia on account of the rush. I know of eight graves at the workings, three more along the road, and eight at and near Wyndham".[27]

The logistics of supporting the rushers drew businessmen who saw opportunities to make a profit from them. Miners needed equipment, food, transport, lodgings and, obviously, somewhere to spend any money they made.

The first town in the Kimberley was already on the west coast. Derby was surveyed and declared a town in 1883. It was a supply and export port for the eight sheep stations that had been carved out of the plains of the west Kimberley[28]. Cattle came when Charlie and Willie MacDonald overlanded a herd 6,000 km from New South Wales in 1885, the same year that saw Charles Hall find his large nugget.

In 1886, the MacDonalds established a cattle station near Fitzroy Crossing and the Leopold Ranges and called it Fossil Downs. The brothers had set out from Goulburn, three years earlier, with seven hundred head of cattle and sixty horses and, after many privations, finally settled with the survivors of the journey: three hundred head of cattle and thirteen horses.

Derby was their nearest and only port. By 1885 the town had a new jetty, warehouses and supply stores, and therefore, coincidentally, it was ready to welcome the waves of miners who arrived en route to the goldfield. Local storekeepers must have rubbed their hands together in glee.

The miners' main problem was distance. There are 550 km of dusty plains, river crossings, and rough limestone country they needed to cross to reach Halls Creek, and many were ill equipped. Some miners came on foot, pushing wheelbarrows, without ever having experienced the conditions found in the North Australian outback before[29].

Help was already at hand. Explorers already knew of the Cambridge Gulf, in the western part of the Kimberley. Phillip Parker King had named it, whilst visiting the area in 1820, on the *Mermaid*. Among others, King had spotted the Ord River, but it was finally named by Alexander Forrest sixty years later.

Another explorer, Harry Stockdale, had been delivered there by ship in 1884, but he lost three of his men during his journey overland back to the Territory, due to the rough Kimberley terrain.

A further help was William 'Potjostler' Carr-Boyd, whom everyone knew was an expert, and his writings. He had bounced back quickly from his losses. On his return to the north, he wrote often to the newspapers, and was interviewed in depth by journalists keen to spread the excitement of the gold rush. On board the *Gambier*, with six horses and enough provisions and stores to get himself to the Elvira River, Carr-Boyd worried about his fellow rushers. He believed that:

> ... many of the men who are starting are doing so in total ignorance of what awaits them when they land from the boat, and that, if they really knew what was before them, they would hesitate before they faced it without proper preparation There will be plenty of gold found, he has no doubt... but anyone starting without at least three months' provisions will render himself liable to great hardship, if not worse[30].

It would not be 'plain sailing'. There was no broad road between Derby and the diggings, as depicted in southern cities, so Carr-Boyd recommended travelling via the Cambridge Gulf:

> ... I choose the Gulf to land at in preference to Derby on account of its greater proximity to the goldfield. By the map I have got, the degrees of latitude make it from 130 to 140 miles from the spot where Durak [sic] landed in August 1882, to the spot where the men are now getting gold on the Elvira, whereas from King's Sound it would be nearly double the distance, about 280 miles or so. Still, I confess, the latter is by all accounts the easier route for any who start to tramp it, but to any one equipped like I am, and personally, I do not think anyone should start who is not so prepared, the shorter route from Cambridge Gulf has no such disadvantages as should operate to deter him from taking it. I expect to find fair travelling for the horses, and to reach the field in from 150 to 200 miles from the Gulf to the Elvira[31].

Cambridge Gulf is a mere 300 km from Halls Creek, so it was a significantly shorter track to the goldfields. If a port town could be established there, its success would be assured.

At least two entrepreneurs recognised the oncoming rush early on, and they knew that the first storeman in position to supply the new arrivals would do well indeed. One was an ex-policeman from the Northern Territory named Augustus Lucanus, and the other was Patrick ('Patsy') Durack, who had been a part of the cattle drive bringing stock to their newly established Carlton Hill and Ivanhoe Stations, in 1882.

Both these men claimed to be the first to set up their businesses.

Wyndham

Lucanus said he arrived in Cambridge Gulf to set up his business three weeks before his rival and had formed his plans long before Hall and Slattery started the rush:

> … In 1883 there was a great talk at Pine Creek, and other Northern Territory goldfields, about a rush to take place in the Kimberley district, where Phil Saunders and Adam Johns had located gold in '81. So, I left the Police Force and went into partnership with W. K. Griffiths and Sydney Hedley to start a store in the Kimberley before the rush set in. The arrangement was that I should go overland. We consulted several explorers, W. O'Donnell, and Carr Boyd, who were at the time in Palmerston, also Saunders and Johns, who advised me to start at the mouth of the Ord River[32].

This is where Leonard Elvey returns to the story. He was the stockman who helped William Butler track down Harry Redford after he had duffed 1,000 cattle from Bowen Downs in central Queensland and driven them to South Australia.

Lucanus and Elvey, with two Aboriginal 'boys'[33] named Captain and Jacky, had the job of taking horses from Yam Creek, on the goldfields south of Port Darwin, overland to the Ord River and Cambridge Gulf.

Lucanus's party was soon joined by an actual boy:

> After camping a few days on this lagoon several niggers came to our camp, relatives of my two boys. Among them was a little boy, Sambo, about five years old. He asked me several times if he could come with us, but I said he was too young, and could not ride. He caught a beautiful Timor pony I had, saddled her, and galloped round the lagoon several times, then pulled up in front of me and said, "Well, boss, you take me now?" Old Captain came up and said, "He alright, boss; I look after him." So, Sambo was one of our party after this[34].

Lucanus's partner, W. K. Griffiths, organised the shipment of stores on a schooner named *Ellerton*. The plan was that it would leave Port Darwin six weeks after Lucanus's horse party and wait for him at the mouth of the Ord River for 14 days. The schooner would also bring some prospectors:

> ... there also were six old prospectors, passengers, to whom I had to give rations for six months, also let them have enough horses and pack saddles to carry their rations and have one of the black boys. We were to go fifty-fifty in the results of their six months' prospecting[35].

The route to Western Australia took Lucanus past Flora River, Delamere Station, VRD, and Wave Hill Stations (then suffering under a plague of rats), before travelling through Jasper Gorge and reaching the Western Australian border. Ord River Station, the only station then in the East Kimberley region, was another 40 km further on. It was owned by Osman and Panton, of Melbourne, and managed by Bob Button. Donald Swan, who appears elsewhere in this text, was employed there at that time. Button was a hospitable host and Lucanus camped with him for a few days. Button gave him some fresh meat and corned beef, and a rough plan of the country.

The travellers had some trouble with the local tribes as they crossed through their lands:

> ... we were aroused at daybreak by our horses stampeding into camp, and niggers howling and jabbering a distance away. Two of the horses were badly speared and had to be destroyed. The blacks got a good reception[36]. They got right into our camp. Spears were flying thickly. My rugs were pinned to the ground in several places by them. I also felt a knock between the shoulder blades, but in the excitement thought it was from a kundy (throwing stick.) After things quieted down I felt for the bruise and found a stone spear head sticking in my back. The shaft must have broken off right away. The head was so deeply embedded that Elvey could not pull it out with his fingers. He had to take the shoeing pincers, with which he finally extracted it. We then washed the wound with hot water and dressed it with carbolic oil, and I was ready to carry on. Although it was a deep and wide gash, my blood was in pretty good order, and it soon healed[37].

It is probably that the tribesmen were reacting to what they thought was a serious threat. One day Lucanus arrived at a billabong full of ducks and other waterfowl. Hunting them would be easy – except local people were already there:

> We went to the lagoon, the blacks disputing our presence by waving us away. As we did not shift, a big black fellow, singled out of the mob, challenged us, shaking his spear at us and yelling. So, Captain stripped all his clothing off, and advanced towards the nigger. When Captain was about 70 yards from him the nigger threw his spear, which Captain cleverly dodged. The nigger shipped his second spear and was just in the act of throwing when Captain smashed his arm with a rifle bullet. Another nigger took his place to have a go at Captain, with the same result. In all eight niggers singled out, and all met with the same fate before they took to their heels, and we had the lagoon to ourselves.

> Soon the ducks settled down. I never saw such a big mob in my life before. About eight yards from the water, we could not see the ground for them. Also, the water was full of them. We camped there. Looking around we saw nigger paths worn in the stony ground between the different lagoons. They must have walked these paths for hundreds of years[38].

When Lucanus arrived at Cambridge Gulf, he found the *Ellerton* already there. His stores were safe, and the party of prospectors[39] he supported were ready to work. Lucanus scouted the area around View Hill, selected a site, and within a week they had built a store and stowed away the goods, including, of course, hogsheads of rum, brandy, and whisky.

Lucanus then took the prospectors upriver to House Roof Hill, which was as far as they could go by boat. They loaded up their horses, which had been cared for by Elvey, and set off for Halls Creek to seek their fortunes. Lucanus returned to his store, ready to welcome more prospectors. He didn't have to wait long:

> In about a fortnight the schooner *Ellerton* arrived again from Port Darwin with some 20 prospectors, also a good Chinese cook and gardener. There was no chance of getting to the goldfields, so they had to camp. They were all well provided with money, so I did good 'biz'[40].

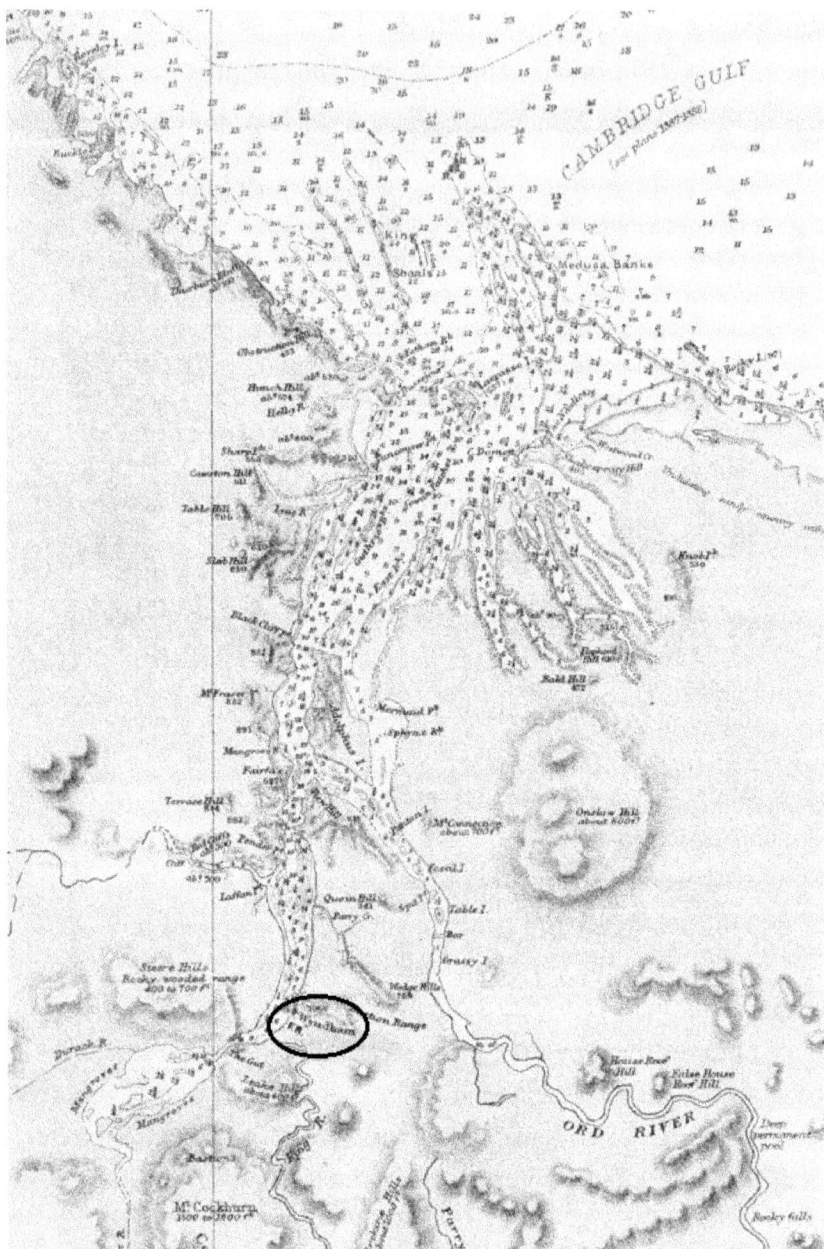

Map 3: When Wyndham was settled in 1886, all that was known of the coast and the lands south was recorded by Commander King (1820), and the few overland explorers like Forrest, Carr-Boyd, and O'Donnell (Admiralty Chart, *Cape Ford to Buccaneer Archipeligo*, 1941).

Lucanus was joined by another storeman:

Another sailing boat arrived, with Mr. Paddy Durack, who
also started a store, and some more prospectors[41].

In 1929, Patsy's son, Patrick (Paddy) Durack (1870-1933) read
the reminiscences Lucanus recorded for the *Daily News* in Perth. His
recollections were different. This inspired him to pen his own story
and it was published by the *Daily News* in Perth in September 1929.
Durack had brought cattle overland on a drive led by his brothers, but
he left them at Victoria River and went to Darwin to purchase stores
and await their arrival in the East Kimberley. Durack's plan was to be
a supplier for both the prospectors and the cattlemen.

In conjunction with the Adcock brothers and Brown we
chartered a large sailing boat called *Lerinda Borstel* to land
me in Cambridge Gulf, and the other members of the party
at Derby in King's Sound. Both parties had large supplies of
stores for new stations which were to be formed when the
cattle arrived from Queensland. The Kimberley goldfields rush
being anticipated, supplies for gold diggers were also loaded by
both parties.

… I was landed at View Hill on September 27, 1885, about
one and a half miles to the east of Land Slip Point in the
estuary of the Ord River. Both sides of the gulf looked dry and
barren, and the captain told me I looked broken-hearted. After
dropping anchor in the gulf, and having no particular place
at which to land, Thomas Hayes, myself, and two Chinamen
went ashore in a small boat to look for water. We found a
pandanus spring three miles east of the ship, at the foot of
View Hill. The spring was half a mile from saltwater marshes
and was not easy to get at. The next day we proceeded in the
boat up West Arm of the Gulf to King River to a place now
known as the Three Mile, in search of water, but failed to find
any, and returned to the ship. The following day we decided
to unload at View Hill, and to carry water from the pandanus
spring in buckets. This work was done by three Chinese cooks
whom we brought from Darwin. After three weeks of water
carrying, we discovered a small spring at low tide on the edge
of the mangroves. This discovery greatly relieved the water
situation, and we made camp 300 yards east, of where the

goods were landed as there was no room for a building at the landing spot. I engraved the name of the ship, the date and year on a large boab tree growing nearby[42].

Only then, according to Patrick Durack, did Augustus Lucanus turn up:

> Three weeks later another schooner owned by W. K. Griffiths, storekeeper of Port Darwin, sailed in with a cargo of stores. He unloaded his goods at our landing. Mr. August Lucanus then came overland and took charge as manager for Mr. Griffiths[43].

Durack and his Chinese companions[44] transported the goods (sugar, flour, tin, and timber) to the chosen site by a canoe they carved out of the soft wood of a boab tree and oars they fashioned from milled timber they had brought with them. The "18ft, by 12ft. by 9ft." store was constructed within a week using this timber, plus mangrove stems felled from forests on Adolphus Island in the gulf, and corrugated iron.

Although their recollections of who arrived first do not coincide, the small community settling on the banks of Cambridge Gulf were not acrimonious rivals. In fact, they got on well, and helped each other out on numerous occasions. They both recall their first Christmas there:

> [Lucanus]: We had a good Christmas – plenty of good food and beer. On Boxing Day, we had sports. Everybody enjoyed himself, so with sports, concerts etc, the time passed quickly[45].

> [Durack]: Christmas time arrived in due course and on Boxing Day we got up some sports, including running, jumping, and shooting at a target at 300 yards. This was won by Lucanus. The 100 yards handicap was won by McKenzie with myself second[46].

In early 1886, the Gulf hosted its first big steamer. The *Catterhun*[47], under Captain Dark, was en route for Hong Kong from Melbourne, and called in to deliver Billy O'Donnell at View Hill. He also brought a large supply of stores, horses, pack saddles, picks, shovels, and gold dishes, which had to be landed in boats. Next came the *Rajputana* from Sydney, bringing Michael and John Durack, with horses and bulls for their new Argyle Station, Kilfoyle's Rosewood Station, and Michael Durack's Lissadell Station. The horses were landed at Land Slip Point, and the stores at View Hill[48]. The British-India steamer, RMS *Quetta*, under Captain Sanders, also called in during those first few months[49].

Among the new arrivals on the *Rajputana* were six women and seven children.

The establishment of cattle stations coincided with the upcoming rush to Halls Creek. Everyone knew the rush was inevitable and the government actively promoted it, hoping to open a lucrative goldfield. In May 1886, John Forrest established Wyndham as the first town in the East Kimberley to bring order to the Cambridge Gulf and ensure the rules were kept. The s.s. *Albany*, under Captain Anton, brought Forrest and several members of Parliament, and a new government resident, Mr. C. D. Price, who was also to be the gold warden and magistrate for the East Kimberley.

A survey party was put to work to mark out the new town, led by Mr. Ranford. They chose the place they called Anton's Landing, after their captain, although there was no fresh water until they dug a well. The town of Wyndham still stands on Anton's Landing.

Recognising their prior settlement, and needing their services, Forrest offered a choice of the newly surveyed blocks to both Lucanus and Durack, so they moved their stores and became the first settlers in the new town[50].

Then, on 19 May 1886, John Forrest stood on the shores of Cambridge Gulf and officially declared the Kimberley Goldfield. The rush was on, and Forrest was proud of his work. He authored a paper that was presented to the Geographical Society of Australasia in July and published widely throughout the colonies. He warned that Wyndham would have little appeal for most people, but it would be an important centre, nevertheless:

> Its geographical position must, to some extent, always mitigate against its being a desirable home for the Anglo-Saxon race,

though it will, I think, be a healthy abode. It is not a climate that one would desire to live in from choice; and I fear, therefore, that the prospects of it becoming the permanent home of a large number of our countrymen in the next few years is not great. It, however, is likely to be the centre of extensive and rich gold mines, which are likely to attract thousands towards them, and will result in the whole country being opened up by telegraphs and railways[51].

Forrest's evaluation of the Kimberley gold prospects had the effect, naturally, of encouraging the rush:

A goldfield has been proclaimed between latitude 16° and 19° south and longitude 126° and 120° east, and a warden and a strong escort are now on their way to the place, ready to take up their duties. The gold has been found in good-sized lumps, the largest, as far as I have learnt, being 19oz., but a great many being in 1oz. and ½oz. pieces. It has been found on the surface, or almost so, and I should say must be close to reefs of very great richness. From the reports of the diggers and other information I have obtained, I have gathered that the gold was easily procured, and that a considerable quantity was obtained in a very short time[52].

Very soon, thousands of men were on their way. They came from all the Australian colonies and New Zealand, most often by ship to Derby or Wyndham. Very few of them had any experience in fossicking for gold, and even fewer were bushmen of any skill. When Warden C.D. Price started touring the goldfields, he found:

There has been a considerable amount of sickness during the past three months fever and ague[53], dysentery, and scurvy being the most prevalent. Many men brought fever in their system and must expect it. But it has been nothing in comparison to what it was on our first reaching the field; great numbers were stricken down, in a dying condition, helpless, destitute of their money, food, or covering, and without mates or friends, simply lying down to die; assistance had to be rendered these[54].

A few miners found payable gold, but most were disappointed. There are no records of exactly how many men went to their graves, and their bones still lie in Old Halls Creek's little cemetery or in lonely bush graves. Some of them died 'like sheep'. One party discovered a man on the track "who had over a pound weight of gold and some sovereigns; but who shot himself rather than endure the misery of existence"[55]. Many wisely turned back after reaching the Kimberley ports, daunted by the long trek in front of them, or by the grey faces of failed miners who returned, destitute, from the fields. Of those who managed the journey, some continued to dig for several years, hoping for success, but "finding, as everybody else did, that though the color [sic] could be got anywhere, it was no diggings"[56].

By the end of the year the rush was over, and most men left in droves. Gold fever encourages men to read any and all positive news through rose-coloured glasses but blinds them to the negative. Many men succumbed, starting as early as June 1886, but even before the rush began, there were others warning that it would be a 'duffer':

> The news sent south is greatly exaggerated, and the diggers are greatly incensed at whoever penned the report! They threaten to burn Deeley's store down if the field turns out a duffer… and if the field turns out a duffer, why the amount of misery cannot be imagined. It is a beastly place to land[57].

Negative stories began appearing more often in the papers across the colonies, even as the rush continued. For example, in October 1886:

> The steamer *Hero* has arrived at Cooktown from Kimberley with 250 return diggers, who speak in unqualified terms of the rush as a duffer[58].

It was even worse a few months later:

> This rush… without doubt the greatest duffer that ever existed, and also the most expensive to get at. I reckon that over £1,000,000 has been expended on it for the magnificent yield of about 300 oz. of gold, or a cost of over £330 for every ounce of gold that has been obtained[59].

But John Forrest continued to talk the goldfields up, no matter what the news. Western Australia needed the rush, so he blamed poor diggers for the problems, and sent more police:

Mr. Forrest, Commissioner of Crown Lands in Western Australia… says that, although the news from Kimberley is bad, there is nothing to be afraid of. A lot of needy people went there in the unfavourable season and had neither money nor food. Those with means will not go up till the needy people have cleared out, as otherwise they will only be carting rations for them, as it is impossible to refuse food[60].

And pity the poor miners who arrived in the 'unfavourable season'. "What use there is in living at all if a man was compelled to stay on here?" wrote one correspondent:

The prospect in store for those who intend remaining over the wet season is anything but an enviable one, and I pity those who may be compelled to stay[61].

The heat and the insects were some of the biggest problems:

… the heat is almost unbearable. At night sleep is banished almost entirely from all unless they chose to drink themselves into a state of obliviousness. Mosquitoes in thousands noiselessly enter your apartment, and, without any warning, swarm down upon their victim, who gets no intimation of their presence until it is felt… Nets are useless, unless made of cheese cloth, and then when drawn loosely round, the heat becomes suffocating.

Then there is the prickly heat, and it is not the ordinary rash with which one is occasionally inflicted in New South Wales, Victoria, and the other colonies, but a mass of sores, which break out all over the body and defies removal by the aid of lotions or soothing oils, and when one gets it, he has to grin and bear his "itch" with the fortitude of a martyr…

The next plague is the flies. If you should by any accident manage to get sleep during the night, immediately you rise you have to battle gamely all day long against flies. Large flies and small flies; the little black pests who never retreat from an attack until killed: the hideous March flies, whose sting is as painful as a wasps; the treacherous sand fly; and the flying ants, which are about night and day; and, in fact, flies of every conceivable colour, size, and nationality are always on the *qui vive*, and attack poor mortals here with a relentlessness which is really awe-inspiring. We are prevented from enjoying our food for them. Soup is ruined, and honey, treacle, porridge, jam, &c., gets thickened; in fact, with every article of food we eat, we have necessarily to consume a certain percentage of flies[62].

Another writer also complained about the insects: "Those who can afford it wear veils, and those who can't, use bad language as a substitute[63]," he wrote.

In a four-month period from June to October in 1887, 2,702 passengers arrived at Wyndham by sea. Many of these moved on to the goldfields directly, although over 1,300 departures meant some diggers were already on their way home, or the wiser new arrivals realised how hard the 'rush' across the Kimberley would be, and so returned with their tails between their legs, back to the comfort of their more southern clime on the very same ship that had brought them.

Arrival

Government resident and warden, C. D. Price, reported two thousand miners in Halls Creek in September 1886, a few weeks before the Ragged Thirteen arrived. The Thirteen had spent weeks in Western Australia about that time, and the Ord River Station manager, Bob Button, had already had a run in with them. Camping nearby on the Ord River, Charles Gaunt said he was a witness to their larceny when they demanded Button kill a bullock for them. He refused, though he did agree to sell them some salt. This they purchased, but naturally, they then helped themselves to the Ord River cattle anyway, and used Button's salt to 'salt-down' the beef that they had not been allowed to purchase:

> … they rode up to the milking yard with their packs, killed a 4-year-old milker's poddy and next day set sail for Hall's Creek[64].

News of their exploits travelled before them, of course, so Constable Troy and his colleagues on the goldfields were keeping a lookout for them:

The police… anticipated their arrival, but evidently the 'Thirteen' guessed what might happen and separated. Split up into twos and threes, what had been a lawless band by weight of numbers became quite tame once the 'Thirteen' were divided[65].

They became as anonymous as the next miner and easily merged with the thousands of hopefuls already there to try their luck. There are no further records of the Ragged Thirteen acting as a gang in Western Australia. However, this did not stop newspaper journalists or correspondents from repeating any story they could find about them over the next few decades. The *Northern Standard* printed a few in 1931:

Arriving there, they sent two of their number to Wyndham for rations, armed with a roll of bad paper. They rung in a lot of it on Lucanus, storekeeper and the hotels, came back and the gang split up, some going to the new finds in W.A., others coming back into the Territory.

They cleaned up a lot of horses belonging to the new chum gold diggers of Hall's Creek but did not touch horses belonging to any man game enough to follow them. They were a petty larceny gang, "Saddle Strap Bushrangers."[66]

Halls Creek, as the Thirteen saw it in 1886, was an ever-increasing camp of canvas tents pitched within walking distance of a government well (which needed locking overnight) and tents that sold grog. The settlement itself was not gazetted as a town until 1897, but mud-brick buildings, including a hospital, post office, police station, several stores, and several hotels[67] were soon constructed[68].

Most miners found 'colour' on their claims, and it seems the Thirteen managed to find enough to keep their interest up for a few months, but nowhere near enough to make it financially worthwhile.

One story suggests that the Thirteen missed a significant find by abandoning one claim too early and allowing it to be taken over by some Chinese diggers, who dug deeper and found a large number of nuggets. The Thirteen are supposed to have been incensed at this, believing the hoard to be rightfully theirs. They then are said to have stolen the cache from the Chinese joss house, where it was hidden[69]. In this tale, this was the end of the gang. They then split the loot and disappeared, either back to the Territory, or to the new goldfields in the south.

The weakness of this story is the mention of Chinese diggers. In fact, there was none in the Kimberley then at all. Three hundred diggers had petitioned the government in 1886 for "the restriction of Chinese immigration, and the exclusion of from the goldfields for three years"[70].

Reports from public meetings, show that the European diggers were at pains to avoid the problems they had experienced in other goldfields, where the Chinese diggers worked harder and longer for less money, and therefore took all 'their' gold.

> The Chinese question is being earnestly discussed, and most urgent appeals made to the Government to pass restrictive measures against the influx of Chinamen. The population seems determined that the Chinese shall not get the upper hand here as they have in Queensland[71].

Chinese diggers were thus excluded from the Western Australian goldfields until at least the 1890s. Clause 3 in the Western Australian Government's *Goldfields Bill* of October 1886, was clear:

> No miner's right, or any lease, license, or permit on any goldfield shall be issued or granted under this Act to any Asiatic or African alien before the expiration of five years from the date of the first proclamation of such goldfield[72].

It was "agreed to without comment" but the Bill went further. Chinese diggers were not allowed to be employed by European miners, either. In clause 8:

> No consolidated miner's right shall authorise the employment... thereof of an Asiatic or African alien on a goldfield[73].

In 1888, controversy arose when Chinese men were employed in the building of a telegraph line across the Kimberley, but it was not until the early 1890s that Chinese labour was actively sought by any mining companies still operating in the Kimberley. The manager of the Ruby Queen Mine, George Wright, needed their help badly. "It seems," he wrote, "that the time has arrived for allowing Chinese labor [sic] on the Kimberley field. Mr. Jephson, Warden, is, I understand, in favor [sic] of this course"[74].

The Ruby Queen was a success for several years. In 1896 they were more than two hundred feet deep, and achieving an ounce per ton[75], but by this time of course, the Ragged Thirteen, and most of the other diggers, were long gone.

The Gang Breaks Up

Finding out what happened to members of the gang after their rampage across country in 1886, was not hard, at least for some of them. Several became legitimate businessmen, cattle station owners, and/or family men. Some chased more gold in the next Western Australian rush, some returned to the Northern Territory, and others went home. Some died young, others lived for decades, but not one was ever brought to account for their behaviour on the trail to Halls Creek, in 1886.

Tom Nugent

Nugent returned to the Territory and continued to work with cattle. On one drive through the Borroloola/McArthur River region, he met a young Garrwa woman named Alice Nampin, who became his life-long companion and the mother of his children, Maudie and Maisie. Children like these – the children of white cattlemen and Aboriginal women – quickly became the backbone of the Territory pastoral industry. In fact, Aboriginal people were integral to the success of cattle farming right across the Top End of Australia. Many were initially reluctant to accept the arrival of white men and their cattle, and resistance was met with enough violence to ensure those that remained were disenfranchised enough to submit to the new regime.

It was an easy decision for a white invader to realise that

Aboriginal people knew their country better than they ever would, and that killing the tribe made no sense. Far better, thought men like Tom Nugent, when starting his own cattle station in 1895, to use them as a work force to look after the cattle, build the yards, clean the houses, tail the horses, and protect the white men. An added advantage of this, was that Aboriginal workers were not required to be paid anything other than a supply of tea, sugar, flour, and tobacco – a situation that continued in the Territory until equal pay was introduced by legislation, in 1968.

Nugent worked on the Overland Telegraph Line for a few years, and this meant regularly travelling his allotted section of the line. While doing so he found an unclaimed patch of pastoral land between Powell's Creek and Tennant's Creek. It contained a delightful, and permanent, spring-fed waterhole in its ranges, and that appealed to him greatly. It lay about 100 km north of Tennant Creek, on the traditional lands of the Warumungu and Warlmanpa people. The freshwater spring was known to them as Punkurr Punkurr, but that was quickly mispronounced as 'Banka Banka'. In 1895, Nugent established Banka Banka Station[76].

Modern travelers through the Territory know Banka Banka, because it is crossed by the Stuart Highway and includes Attack Creek, where John McDouall Stuart was turned around by 'bold and daring' Aboriginal men, during his 1860 attempt to cross the continent[77].

Tom and Alice are known to have rescued several Aboriginal children who were either orphaned or homeless. One, a little boy from Borroloola, named George, grew up to be a cattlemen and station manager – entrusted by Nugent to take on Buchanan Downs Station[78] when he purchased it in 1902. Nugent spoke to the *Australian Star* newspaper about George in 1907:

> In 1884 I came across a tiny little black toddler, just able
> to crawl on all fours. He was a few months old and had
> apparently been lost. When I came across him he was making
> for a waterhole. I took him home and reared him on mare's

milk, and he is the man now in charge of Buchanan Downs[79].

Another foundling was Kathleen O'Shea (Katie). Nugent had come across her after a massacre of Anula people near Borroloola. Billy Linklater recorded the story:

> ... A punitive expedition had wiped out the adults involved
> [in a murder], but Tom discovered a forgotten baby girl. He
> took the tiny creature, whom he dubbed Kathleen O'Shea,
> to Mary, a responsible lubra, and gave instructions that she
> should be looked after. Safely in the waggon, she reached
> Banka Banka with the rest of Tom's Aboriginal retainers[80].

Because the Overland Telegraph Line crossed the station, regular visitors of maintenance teams and travellers called in, even in the early days. This gave the station customers who could buy the beef and goods that Nugent was able to keep in a store. One annual visitor was John Archibald Graham Little, the long-serving Post and Telegraph Superintendent based in Darwin. He recorded:

> Mr. Thomas Nugent has formed a nice station at Banka
> Banka; a small garden at the homestead yields an ample supply
> of all kinds of vegetables of remarkable size and quality[81].

Lindsay Crawford also visited during the time he was a linesman based at Powell Creek Telegraph Station, about 150 km north of Banka Banka. Despite being away working cattle at the time, Crawford, then the manager, remembered the Ragged Thirteen's raid on Victoria River Downs Station in 1886. But time heals all wounds and, according to Ernestine Hill, he and Nugent "buried the hatchet of those *borrowed* horseshoes in laughter"[82], and "heartily toasted" the memory of the Ragged Thirteen.

Figure 14: Banka Banka Station, 1900 (SLSA B-24217).

Figure 15: Tom Nugent's grave. Nugent died at the Tennant Creek Telegraph Station in 1911.

Tom Nugent, aka Holmes, died at Tennant's Creek Telegraph Station in 1911 of dropsy[83]. His grave lies behind a wire fence in the grounds of the station, next to the grave of a telegraph linesman named Archibald Cameron, who died in 1903.

Sandy MacDonald

Figure 16: Alexander Sandy MacDonald c 1910 (NTRS 3833-P1_Unit Id 14 Item ASTS 882).

Two of the gang, Sandy MacDonald, and James Woodford, riding together, returned to the Territory and followed a new rush, this time to Central Australia. At first they were after rubies, but that rush fizzled out quickly when the gemstones proved to be garnets. Then gold was discovered near a waterhole the Arrernte called Arltunga, in 1887. For the next few decades, miners lived under canvas in a community spread across spinifex covered hills in the East MacDonnell Ranges. There were not many of them. After the initial rush of an unknown number of men, by 1902 there was a population of just 40 men who were struggling to survive through slow and laborious work (they were counted by Government Geologist H.Y.L Brown in 1902 during one of his inspections via camel[84]).

Arltunga was central Australia's first town[85]. It lay 110 km east of the Alice Springs Telegraph Station. In the beginning, the miners walked or rode the 1500+km from Port Augusta or Adelaide, following the Overland Telegraph Line. But, after 1890, the railway line ran as far as Oodnadatta, some 600 km south, so the miners could travel to the railhead by *The Ghan* train, and walk from there, overland to Arltunga. Camel trains brought in supplies, but they were very slow. It took a week for them to walk from the Alice Springs Telegraph Station, for instance, sometimes in temperatures that approached 48 degrees Centigrade.

Some overlanders, like Sandy Myrtle MacDonald and James

Woodford, arrived from the north. MacDonald's eventual success in Arltunga came not from mining, but from other miners. Before that, however, he followed another new rush to Western Australia in 1894, taking a draft of horses from Oodnadatta to Coolgardie. It is not known how long he scratched the dirt or how successful he was at mining, but he was soon back at Arltunga. In 1903, he was listed as a horse dealer on the electoral roll in Oodnadatta and he also held a store and slaughtering licence at Winnecke's Depot at Arltunga from 1904 to 1910[86]. He then opened the Glencoe Hotel at the crossroads of the township in September 1910. The remains of the hotel can still be seen at the crossroads as you approach the old town. As a garrulous publican, MacDonald enjoyed the company of miners and drank many of the profits, getting very fat in the process. His obituary suggests he weighed 23 stone (146 kg)[87], although others say 28 stone (177 kg).

Once settled back in Arltunga, he married an Arrernte woman named Korulya. Together they raised a daughter named Myrtle[88]. As the pub's owner and therefore a community leader, MacDonald hosted Arltunga's first church service, run by Presbyterian Patrol Padre Robert Plowman, on 29 June 1914. Plowman recorded in his diary his shock at the yellow meat being served in the Glencoe Hotel. MacDonald had sprinkled it with 'Insectibane,' a powdered insecticide used to kill insects.

"It keeps the flies off," MacDonald told him[89].

James Woodford

Jim Woodford also lived in Arltunga for many years. Some of his income came from the search for and sale of meteorites and some from mining leases he held at Paddy's Hole, Arltunga. One meteorite he brought in was the largest found in South Australia:

> … Mr. James Woodford, of Arltunga, has brought to the
> office of the Commissioner of Crown Lands a mass of iron,
> weighing about 40 lb., which on examination proved to be a

meteorite. This meteorite was found by Mr. D. Pedler, near Paddy's Hole, about two miles from the Arltunga cyanide works. Near the foot of a range, Pedler noticed a peculiar hole in the soft ground and looking down he saw a scar or mark along it leading to the hole. He opened the hole out, and at a depth of 5 ft. from the surface found the meteorite[90].

Woodford must have been pleased when the meteorite was sold:

The Arltunga meteorite, which was recently left at the Crown Lands Office by Mr. James Woodford, has been purchased by the Museum authorities... Mr. H. Y. L. Brown (Government Geologist), by whom it was brought under notice of Professor Stirling (Director of the Museum), has arranged for an analysis to be made at the School of Mines[91].

In later years, Woodford found employment, ironically for an ex-bushranger, as a warder in the Stuart (Alice Springs) gaol, and at the Arltunga lock-up, where he watched prisoners for the police. In 1919, Woodford also held a store-keeper's licence, but he kept mining and was an advocate for the construction of a railway from Oodnadatta to Arltunga to a visiting public works committee in 1921.

Woodford remained in Arltunga until he died, sitting in a chaff-bag armchair, in September 1921, aged sixty-six. His death, most probably of heart failure, came thirty-five years after he had ridden with the Ragged Thirteen. His grave still stands in the lonely Arltunga Crossroads Cemetery, protected by a hefty rock wall.

Bob Anderson

Robert George Anderson's legacy is larger than most. After returning to Queensland and spending some years driving a bullock team throughout Western Queensland and working as a butcher in Camooweal[92], he married Emma Carrington from Cloncurry and together they had fourteen children (5 sons and 9 daughters, the last of whom was born in 1916). The family moved to Urandangi in the early 1900s, and Anderson managed the store until 1913, when he established Tobermory Station on land that he had already been running his cattle on for several years. He built a magnificent two-

Figure 17: Robert George Anderson, 1857-1923 (c 1910, Ref: Anderson family, Queensland).

storey homestead called Tobermory House in 1914. A part of it still exists, near the border of Queensland and the Northern Territory.

Many of Bob and Emma Anderson's descendants remain a large part of the cattle station folk still working across Queensland, from Longreach to Boulia.

Unfortunately, Bob was killed in a fall from a buggy in January 1923, aged 65. There is a memorial at the site of the fall, and Anderson's bones lie in Urandangi Cemetery. Like Tom Nugent, he is remembered a respected pioneer pastoralist. An obituary in the *Daily Mail* in July 1923 made no mention of his wild days in the Ragged Thirteen:

> Mr. Robert Anderson, a well-known Gulf and Georgina River Pioneer, passed away at his station, Tobermory, on the Queensland Northern Territory border. Deceased was born in Scotland but came to this state at an early age. In the eighties, he was engaged in carrying to Normanton and Burketown then the ports for all the country right to Boulia and Central Australia. Eventually he went to Camooweal, where he married, and then he ran a store at Urandangie [sic] for many years. While there he took up Tobermory and built one of the finest homesteads in the north-west, which he fitted up with electric light, refrigerating plant, and had many windmills. Deceased was 65 years of age, over 20 of which wore spent on the Georgina River. He leaves a widow and grown-up family[93].

Hugh Campbell

Hugh Campbell started work as a camp cook for Gordon Buchanan on Flora Valley Station, near Katherine, but became anhidrotic in 1908 – which meant he was unable to sweat. This condition can be inherited, but also caused by alcoholism, diabetes, or a number of other problems. Whatever the cause, as he grew ill, Campbell went home to his native Scotland, and it is believed that he died soon after he arrived.

'Wonoka' Jack and George Brown

The brothers quickly left mining behind and took a contract to build the police station, post office and general store at Halls Creek[94]. The brothers were then employed by Bernard Murphy, who by then ran the Sportsman Hotel and Pioneer Cash Store on the Katherine River[95]. Murphy was the 'indefatigable secretary' of the Katherine Racing Club in Katherine. The Brown brothers were pit sawmillers for as long as the work lasted and afterwards, they headed out to nearby Maude Creek to try their hands, once again, at gold mining. Unfortunately, Jack grew ill and returned to South Australia, only to die soon after of hydatids.

As for George Brown, there was a man of that name who was the station master at Pine Creek for many years – though perhaps it is fanciful to think he was the same George Brown who was a member of the Ragged Thirteen[96].

'New England' Jack Woods

Woods continued to work in and around goldfields in Western Australia, butchering other people's cattle and sheep and selling the meat, possibly with Tommy the Rag working as a partner for a few years. He became well known enough to be recalled by John Meiklejohn in the *Western Mail* in 1937:

> Jack was at times butcher, digger, bushman, sly grog seller or politician. He came overland from Queensland for the Kimberley rush and was reputed to be a member of the "Ragged Thirteen." Whether this was correct or not, it is a fact that he commenced butchering early in Kimberley.
>
> From there he followed all the rushes through the Nor'-West, Murchison. Coolgardie and outlying fields. There was

frequently a strong suspicion as to the source of his meat supply, but nothing wrong was ever proved against him. He was a true bush lawyer, and openly boasted that he preferred a crooked deal to a straight one. There was more thrill, he said, in the former. But money was only a medium to get drink- which was his great weakness.

At Mt. Magnet, it was Woods who bought the consignment of liquor, afterwards called "Solomon's Solution," which upset the camp so much that the crowd would have lynched old Solomon, the seller, if they had caught him. When Gardiner got lost in the bush and was nearly all in through thirst after he found the "Star of the East," Jack Woods found him and nursed him back to health. Gardiner showed his appreciation by giving Jack a half share with him in the mine. It all went the usual way.

When "two-up" schools were in session, Jack was a regular attender. If he took the kip, his actions were always closely watched, as he was reputed to have nimble fingers. It might have been in his case, "Give a dog a bad name, and you may as well hang him," because Jack was never detected doing tricks with the pennies.

He opened a hop beer shanty near Fly Spot Flat near the end of '92, which proved a great convenience to the camp on more than one occasion. One of the first at Broad Arrow, he supplied the camp with fresh mutton. His shop was a bough shed and a few Aboriginals were always present as helps in his work. It was a striking picture with Jack in the foreground, his waist belt strung with heavy gold pouches, and his trouser pockets bulging grotesquely with other gold "chammies."

"It's a leg you'll be wantin?" Jack would say to a customer. "Now here's a beauty!" and he would hook one on to a handspring balance, hold the dial close to the customer's eyes, pull the bottom of the leg steadily with his left hand and, taking a squint himself at the dial "That's 81/2 pounds! Say 8/6." And if the customer had not observed the fraud Jack would get 2lb. more weight the best of it. He got a warning about those methods, however, which obliged him to be more careful.

He had a weakness for horses. He loved them and tended

them well. When Tim Creed perished through thirst near the White Feather, Jack found the dead man's two beautiful grey horses quietly grazing in the vicinity. He promptly took charge of them, informed the Progress Committee what he had done and immediately cleared off with them.

Weeks afterwards a police messenger located Woods at some distant digging and demanded possession of the horses. Jack replied by making out such a formidable account for looking after the nags that the police allowed him to retain them rather than contest his claim. He thus obtained two beautiful horses without any cash outlay.

Jack was thin and scraggy, his hair and beard mostly unkempt, and he generally appeared unwashed. It was, consequently, a surprise to hear this scare-crow address meetings. He had a wonderful delivery, never halted for a word, language correct, and his argument sound. That is where he scored in politics...

The last seen of Woods, he was heading away outback when Coolgardie became too civilised for him, and he has never since been heard of. In spite of his questionable business methods, Jack was lavishly generous to any person who stood in need of help. His name will linger in the memories of old-timers as one of the outstanding characters who figured in the history of the early goldfields.

John Meiklejohn, Nedlands[97].

Meiklejohn was wrong about Woods' disappearance in the bush because he is known to have returned to his home and family in New England, where he lived out the rest of his days.

According to Linklater, Woods visited Tom Nugent at Banka Banka, and stayed for a few months, in 1900. Many a night might have been spent yarning about old times.

Tommy the Rag

Tommy the Rag remains the most anonymous of the Thirteen. He followed Jack Woods to the new goldfields at Coolgardie in Western Australia, and quickly disappeared from the record. This would have been a simple thing to do as he only had to call himself by his real

name and no one would have been the wiser. Eddie Webber discovered
that he had also been called 'Tommy the Lag' and that his journey to
Coolgardie was not without incident:

> On his arrival in the Top End, Tommy admitted to having
> served time, and with no Christian name, was christened
> Tommy the Lag. He threw his fortunes in with the Ragged
> Thirteen and as the goldfields at Hall's Creek petered out,
> he and three other companions set out for Coolgardie. This
> time he was well provisioned, and the country had just
> experienced rain. However, two hundred miles into the trip,
> tragedy struck. Although their horses were hobbled, they lost
> two overnight and wasted two days searching. With the loss
> of horses, they were forced to leave rations and some of their
> water behind. They had ridden past the last known waterholes
> and the group quarrelled over the lost horses. Tommy and
> Alec Smith split from the others, struggling on surviving by
> boiling water from a polluted rock hole. Alec Smith's horse
> collapsed into a hidden gully and rolled killing him. Tommy
> had to shoot the horse to put him out of his misery and buried
> the horse and rider in a common grave. The shot that killed
> the horse also frightened Tommy's horse, which galloped away.
> Tommy trudged on, finally limping into an outlying miner's
> camp almost perishing, out of strength and possessions, but
> surviving to become part of the Coolgardie hessian city[98].

Jim Carmody

Jim Carmody, the last of the Thirteen to join the gang on that fateful
day at Abraham's Billabong, returned to the Northern Territory but,
unfortunately, did not last long. He drowned in the Katherine River
in 1889, tangled in his fishing line:

> Some slight particulars of the drowning of James Carmody
> last week are to hand. It appears that he left the Sportsmans
> Hotel at 6 o'clock a. m. on the 23rd January to go fishing
> in the Katherine River. Being still absent at breakfast time,
> someone went in search of him, with the result that he was
> found drowned in the river with a fishing line tangled all
> round his body. The supposition is that he had climbed out
> on an overlapping branch to fish and had either fallen or

been dragged into the water, where he got mixed up with the line, and so was unable to save himself. Carmody was a fair swimmer, we hear, so that under ordinary circumstances he would hardly be drowned in eight feet of water quite close to the bank of the river[99].

As Carmody was staying in the Sportsmans Hotel, he was no doubt still in touch with Wonaka Jack and George Brown, who were sawmilling in Katherine around that time. Perhaps it was one of them who went looking for their old friend when he had not returned. Carmody was buried in the Knotts Crossing Cemetery, a rarely visited graveyard near Knott's Crossing, which contains the graves of at least twenty-nine of the early pioneers of the Katherine region.

Jack Dalley

Jack Dalley, who was originally a farmer in the railway gauge-changing town of Terowie in South Australia, finally settled near Cloncurry, where he continued with cattle droving. He rarely appears in the records after that, but once he made the newspapers through a little carelessness, in 1928:

> Last Monday afternoon what might have been a serious accident occurred in Ramsay Street, when a man named Jack Dalley was knocked down and rendered unconscious by a motor car, driven by a lady. The Ambulance were quickly on the scene and removed the injured man to the hospital, suffering from slight concussion. He is now out of the institution[100].

According to Ernestine Hill, "Dalley became a leading townsman of Cloncurry and when eager, young reporters came for his reminiscences as a member of the Ragged Thirteen, he threatened them with a rifle."

Dalley married and he and his wife raised two sons, both of whom also became drovers. One of them, George, was killed after a fall from a truck in 1937[101].

Jack was over seventy when he died.

'Larrikin Bill' Smith and Jim Fitzgerald

These two may have given up mining for good. 'Larrikin' Bill Smith and Jim Fitzgerald had such common names they could easily drop from the historical record.

Ernestine Hill suggested "Larrikin Jack Smith [sic] was one of the first in the golden hills of New Guinea,"[102] although she gave no evidence and made an error in his name. It is more likely that they returned to a life in the saddle and stock work on remote stations and, like a thousand others, drifted in anonymity. There is, however, a suggestion from the *Times* in 1928 that Jim Fitzgerald ended his days in a Roman Catholic home for the aged in Western Australia[103].

And that was it! The members of the Ragged Thirteen were never arrested for the crimes they committed in 1886. Allegedly, they were guilty of crimes ranging from assault and horse theft to petty thievery, outright robbery and passing dud cheques, but they got clean away…

As A.N.M. wrote for *The Chronicle* in 1935:

… Although one may be licensed to romance, one must refute the tall tales still told of the terrible 'Ragged Thirteen'. The band certainly existed and caused a great deal of bother to many station managers and proprietors of wayside shanties; but apart from hard drinking, 'lifting' horses, and taking food by force, the 'Ragged Thirteen' did little else to merit the reputation they have gained[104].

Or, as the *Old Timer* put it in 1936:

… in reality they were just a crowd of rough bush men, who relied upon weight of numbers to get them what they wanted, whether it was drink or food. Although outside the law and proved horse-stealers, the 'Thirteen' did not resort to murder. If they did shoot a few Myall blacks, it was as a means of self-preservation[105].

Endnotes

1 Jones, 2004.

2 Lewis, 2004.

3 *Evening News* (Sydney), 14 September 1883, page 2.

4 *Queenslander* (Brisbane), 22 September 1883, page 483.

5 In 1861, the giant northwest pearl oyster was discovered in Roebuck Bay by the crew of the *Dolphin*. In 1879 Charles Harper promoted Roebuck Bay as a port for a pearling industry and the first ships arrived with pearl diving equipment in 1881. There was therefore transport available between the bay and Perth.

6 *Argus* (Melbourne) 30 May 1884, page 3.

7 *Northern Territory Times and Gazette*, 13 October 1883.

8 *Argus* (Melbourne), 12 January 1884. For O'Donnell's full report in two parts see, the Argus of 5 January 1884 page 5, and 12 January 1884. page 13.

9 *Argus* (Melbourne), 31 January 1884, page 9.

10 *Argus* (Melbourne),12 January 1884, page 13.

11 *Argus* (Melbourne) 15 January 1884, page 7.

12 *Argus* (Melbourne), 31 January 1884, page 9.

13 Playford and Ruddock 1985.

14 *Daily News* (Perth), 29 September 1885, page 3: Report of the Kimberley Prospectors.

15 *Daily News* (Perth,), 11 May 1886, page 3: News of the Day.

16 *Herald* (Fremantle), 26 June 1886, page 6: This Week.

17 Unfortunately for Hall and his partner Slattery, the government decided the condition of 10,000 ounces had not been met, and they were awarded just £500 for their efforts in 1888. The widow of the Irish geologist, Hardman, was also awarded £500. Phil Saunders, who with Adam Johns, had confirmed the existence of 'colour', was rejected for the £5,000 reward as well, but an appeal to the Minister for Mines, twenty years later, produced a result. By then, he was 66 years old and working a small gold show, with minimal returns, near Mt Ida (86 km north-west of Menzies, Western Australia). The Mount Ida Progress Association asked that Saunders be granted an appropriate annuity by the Government because 'the old gentleman is now rapidly declining and almost blind' and that he would appreciate receiving appropriate relief to assist him when 'his life is apparently very near its close'. This moving appeal had the desired effect, and Saunders was granted a government pension of £75 per year. If he was indeed close to death in 1907, he recovered well after receiving the annuity and lived for another 24 years, dying in 1931 at the age of 90. Too old to mine, he spent the last few years of his life making hats on one of the Western Australian goldfields (*Northern Territory Times*, 17 January 1928, page 6).

18 *Herald* (Fremantle), 26 June 1886, page 3.

19 *Illustrated Sydney News*, 15 June 1886, page 8, The Kimberley Gold Rush.

20 *Daily Telegraph* (Sydney), 24 May 1886, page 5: The Kimberley Gold rush.

21 *Daily Telegraph* (Sydney), 24 May 1886, page 5: The Kimberley Gold rush.

22 Lucanus called her Mrs. McQuirter (*Daily News*, 28 August 1929, page 6.)

23 August Lucanus *Daily News*, 28 August 1929, page 6.

24 *Northern Territory Times and Gazette*, 3 July 1886, page 3.

25 August Lucanus *Daily News*, 28 August 1929, page 6.

26 August Lucanus *Daily News*, 28 August 1929, page 6. Note that the name Pompey does not appear in the team list – he may have had other names.

27 *West Australian*, 27 January 1887, page 3.

28 This started in 1880, when the Murray Squatting Company established a sheep station at Yeeda, 45 km from Derby. The Derby landing port landed the first cargo in 1881, from *The Ruby* under Captain Pemberton Walcott.

29 Playford, 2005.

30 *Brisbane Courier*, 25 May 1886, page 6.

31 *Brisbane Courier*, 25 May 1886, page 6.

32 Augustus Lucanus, *Daily News* (Perth), 24 August 1929, page 6: Goldfields of the North.

33 In the parlance of the 1800s, Aboriginal workers were called 'boys', and Aboriginal people in general 'niggers' – a word which today carries so much weight it is rarely heard in Australia.

34 Augustus Lucanus, *Daily News* (Perth), 24 August 1929, page 6: Goldfields of the North.

35 Augustus Lucanus, *Daily News* (Perth), 24 August 1929, page 6: Goldfields of the North.

36 Euphemisms like a 'good reception', 'taught a lesson', or 'they were dispersed' almost always meant that Aboriginal people were shot – wounded, or more likely, killed. After some massacres many men, women and children, the bodies were burned, eg Forrest River, see Green 1995.

37 Augustus Lucanus, *Daily News* (Perth), 26 August 1929, page 6: Goldfields of The North.

38 Augustus Lucanus, *Daily News* (Perth), 26 August 1929, page 6: Goldfields of The North.

39 Julius Anderson, Jack Cameron, Dave McClellan (brother-in-law to 'Truthful' James), Sorenson, E. Walsh, Bob McPhee, Fullerton, and H. Howe (Lucanus 1929).

40 Augustus Lucanus, *Daily News* (Perth) 27 August 1929, page 5: Goldfields Of The North.

41 Augustus Lucanus, *Daily News* (Perth) 27 August 1929, page 5: Goldfields Of The North.

42 Patrick (Paddy) Durack, *Daily News* (Perth), 25 September 1929, page 9.

43 Patrick (Paddy) Durack, *Daily News* (Perth), 25 September 1929, page 9.

44 The Chinese men are rarely named, but one of them was called Ah Suey.

45 Augustus Lucanus, *Daily News* (Perth), 27 August 1929, page 5.

46 Patrick (Paddy) Durack, *Daily News* (Perth), 25 September 1929, page 9.

47 The *Catterthun* sank during a storm in 1895 near Point Stephens N.S.W. with the loss of 54 passengers and crew.

48 Patrick (Paddy) Durack, *Daily News* (Perth), 25 September 1929, page 9.

49 RMS *Quetta* was wrecked on the Queensland coast in 1890, killing 134 of its 292 passengers. It remains Queensland's worst maritime disaster.

50 Patrick Durack, *Daily News* (Perth), 28 September 1929, page 9: Pioneering the East Kimberley, Stirring Incidents of Long Ago.

51 *Brisbane Courier*, 9 July 1886, page 3.

52 *Brisbane Courier*, 9 July 1886, page 3.

53 'Ague' was the name for the symptoms of malaria.

54 *West Australian* (Perth) 17 August 1887, page 3.

55 *Evening News* (Sydney, N.S.W.), 20 October 1886, page 5: *Back From The Grave — or Kimberley An Unmitigated Duffer.*

56 *Evening News* (Sydney, N.S.W.), 20 October 1886, page 5: *Back From The Grave — or Kimberley An Unmitigated Duffer.*

57 D. Chambers, *Ovens and Murray Advertiser* (Beechworth, Vic.) 31 July 1886, page 2.

58 *Newcastle Morning Herald and Miners' Advocate*, 11 October 1886, page 5.

59 *Queenslander*, 22 January 1887, page 134, *The Kimberley.*

60 *Evening News* (Sydney, N.S.W.), 20 October 1886, page 5: *Back From The Grave — or Kimberley An Unmitigated Duffer.*

61 *Newcastle Morning Herald and Miners' Advocate* (N.S.W.), 18 February 1887, page 8: Wyndham, the Pioneer Township.

62 *Newcastle Morning Herald and Miners' Advocate* (N.S.W.), 18 February 1887, page 8: Wyndham, the Pioneer Township.

63 *Northern Territory Times and Gazette*, Special Correspondent. 21 August 1886, page 2. (I suspect the author to be Alfred Searcy).

64 *Northern Standard*, 18 September 1931, page 4.

65 A.N.M. *Chronicle* (Adelaide), 24 October 1935, page 15.

66 *Northern Standard*, 18 September 1931, page 4.

67 The three hotels at Halls Creek in the 1890s were Court Hotel, Brand's Hotel and Kimberley Hotel.

68 Once the rush had passed, Halls Creek hung on as a commerce and trade centre to service the dwindling number of mines. Then the town was bypassed by the highway in 1949, so it was moved 15 kilometres to take advantage of the traffic. The original town is now called Old Halls Creek.

69 Cook, 2010.

70 *The Ballarat Star*, 6 July 1886, Page 4 *The Kimberley Goldfields.*

71 *Australian Town and Country Journal* (Sydney) 17 July 1886, page 24, *The Miner.*

72 *The West Australian*, 3 Apr 1896, page 5, *Kimberley.*

73 *The West Australian*, 3 Apr 1896, page 5, *Kimberley.*

74 *Geraldton Murchison Telegraph* (WA), 24 July 1894, page 3, *The Miner.*

75 *The West Australian*, 3 Apr 1896, page 5, *Kimberley.*

76 Marked on an 1895 map as also called Kadjinburra (see Purvis 1946-8).

77 The current station also hosts travelling campers and motel guests who come to see the old, heritage listed, mudbrick homestead and remnants of a World War Two

staging camp.

78 Buchanan Downs Station lies on the Buchanan Highway, west of Katherine, nearly 600 km from Banka Banka.

79 *Australian Star* (Sydney), 29 October 1907, page 5.

80 Linklater and Tapp (1967).

81 Extracts from Mr Little's Diary, *Northern Territory Times and Gazette*, 16 March 1900, page 3.

82 Ernestine Hill, in *Cavaliers of Gold*.

83 Oedema, or swelling under the skin.

84 Jines, 1987.

85 The town of Stuart, now called Alice Springs, was declared in 1888.

86 Holmes, 1980.

87 *Northern Territory Times and Gazette*, 2 August 1919, page 16.

88 Myrtle MacDonald later worked at The Bungalow in Alice Springs, helping look after the children of mixed descent who lived there, many of whom were 'stolen' from their Aboriginal families, although some were sent there voluntarily by station folk for the children's education. Myrtle herself had seven children and many of her descendants still live around Alice Springs and in Newcastle N.S.W.

89 Bucknall, 2008.

90 *Evening Journal* (Adelaide), 23 November 1908, page 1.

91 *Register*, 2 December 1908, page 6.

92 Sandra Anderson, the family's genealogist, Queensland. Personal communication, August 2024.

93 *Daily Mail* (Brisbane), Thursday 5 July 1923, page 12: *Obituary*.

94 This emphasises their anonymity as far as their bushranging careers went – their crimes must have been unknown.

95 *Northern Territory Times and Gazette*, 19 June 1891, page 3.

96 Webber, December 2022.

97 *Western Mail* (Perth), 15 October 1936, page 11, by John Meiklejohn.

98 Webber, 2022.

99 *North Australian*, 2 February 1889, page 2.

100 *Townsville Daily Bulletin*, 17 November 1928, page 14.

101 *Townsville Daily Bulletin*, 17 November 1928, Page 2: Cloncurry Notes. I am assuming that George Dalley was Jack's son. There was a brother mentioned by this source, working on Brunette Downs Station. There are three Dalleys, including George, in the Cloncurry Cemetery, but no mention of Jack. Kate Dalley, who died in 1922, mother of John (died 1975 Mt Isa) who fought in World War 1, is likely to have been Jack's wife.

102 Ernestine Hill, *Daily Mercury*, Mackay, Qld., 20 December 1938.

103 *Northern Territory Times*, 17 January 1928, page 6.

104 A.N.M. *The Chronicle* (Adelaide), 24 October 1935, page 15.

105 'Old Timer', *The Chronicle* (Adelaide), 22 October 1936, page 16.

Chapter 4
Hunted... or not

Police were few and far between in the Northern Territory bush in the 1880s. There were a few lonely outposts, like Roper Bar, Borroloola, and the Shackle, but they were usually staffed by just two mounted constables. Mostly, they had a beat that covered thousands of square kilometres, so, when 'on patrol', the constables could be away from their stations for weeks at a time.

The Ragged Thirteen drew the attention of the police, of course. Unfortunately, the source of the information about their response mostly comes from books written decades later, by Customs Officer Alfred Searcy.

'Unfortunately,' because although Searcy authored several books on his time in the Territory, they vary so much in their level of truth that anything he wrote must be taken with a grain of salt. One of his yarns told of Mounted Constable Donegan's capture of the Thirteen. M.C. Mick Donegan really did transfer to the McArthur Region and Borroloola in August 1886[1] and Searcy spent time in the same area for at least some of that year, so the timing is right, if nothing else[2]. The following story appeared in Searcy's memoir *By Flood and Field*, though Donegan was given the name 'O'Donohue'. It was reprinted as a true story by a number of newspapers, in the early part of the twentieth century[3]:

> When at the shanty at Abraham's Billabong, the keeper
> informed us that word had come from the Bar (Roper) that
> a gang of cowardly ruffians, known as 'The Ragged Thirteen,'

were making their way to Kimberley 'on the nod,' that is, helping themselves to cattle from the stations, food from travellers and shanties, and used their revolvers when resisted. He greatly feared a visit, which, he subsequently received – the scoundrels leaving him nothing but what he stood up in, and that, in the tropics, is precious little.

All went well with us until within about ten miles of the Bar, which we hoped to make after our mid-day camp, when we encountered a number of villainous-looking creatures, travelling on foot.

"The Ragged Thirteen, by Jingo," whispered O'Donohue. Then "Good day, mates," in his hearty Irish way.

"Good day," growled one of the men, who appeared to be the leader. "Who are you fellows, and where are you bound for? Long journey, by the looks of it. You've a nice lot of horses."

These remarks were sandwiched with language that proved the speaker adept in the use of oaths. O'Donohue simply said, "Free country, chaps, isn't it? A fellow can travel where he likes, can't he?"

"Don't know so much about that. But who and what are you?" again asked the leader.

"Well, if you are really anxious to know, we are policemen, bound for the McArthur."

"O, so you are traps, are you?" sneered he. "Traps going to the McArthur? O, what a choice time you will have!"

"Guess we can take care of ourselves," said O'Donohue.

"Do you think you could collar us fellers?"

"Well, if it were necessary, I daresay I could manage," said O'Donohue in a casual way. "But come, mates, let's have a billy of tea and some tucker. You'll find it better than talking tommyrot. I want to get to the Bar this evening."

The saddles and packs were then taken off the horses, and they were allowed to browse around. The billy was soon boiling and all busy with tea, salt meat and damper, when O'Donohue muttered (loud enough to be heard by all): "Where the deuce is my tobacco?" at the same time looking around. "O, yes I must have left it in my saddle pouch."

With that he got up and moved towards the saddle, but

quickly wheeling round, revolver in hand, commanded the crowd to hold up their hands, which order made them gape in astonishment. However, they reluctantly obeyed; and what paws they were! I then disarmed them and stepped to my mate's side with revolver drawn.

The man who had spoken wanted to know what it all meant. For answer O'Donohue told him to shut his mouth, or he would find a gag that would prevent him from doing so. He then ordered them to rise and form into a line, at the same time informing them that he was going to take them to the Bar on the off chance of friends there wanting to see them. Some looked sick at the news, while others laughed at the idea of "two traps collaring the whole bloomin' lot of 'em."

I certainly thought my mate had taken on a big contract and was wondering how he proposed preventing them from bolting, when, as if divining my thoughts, he told me to cut off their braces, straps, and buttons.

For the life of me I couldn't help laughing outright when their breeches began to slip; and, while it would probably have given them the greatest pleasure to have cut the throats of the pair of us, they laughed too.

"All done?" inquired O'Donohue. "All adrift," I replied.

"Now chaps," he said; "you may use your hands, for I guess you will need them. I fancy you'll find it dashed poor business trying to bolt with your bags round your heels and if any refuse to move on or give trouble I'll have their boots off and leave them here."

O'Donohue then asked for his horse, and while he mounted, I was in evidence with my "little orator." When nicely seated, he gave the order to march, and away went the miserable devils in the direction of the Bar.

When I joined my mate he said that as the gang evidently meant mischief, he thought he would have the first say. He expected he would have to release them at the Bar, as none of those robbed would spare the time that would be necessary for their trial.

"But I guess," he went on, "the Bar beauties will see that we have some grit in us; and the game is worthwhile as an object lesson."

Just before sundown we arrived at our destination. There were many drovers, overlanders, and others in camp, and our cavalcade created much excitement as it passed along, many inquiries being made as to what the "pinks" had been up to.

The police troopers soon joined us, giving us a hearty welcome. When O'Donohue explained matters, they looked serious, then annoyed, and finally burst out laughing as if it were the greatest joke in the world. Then the crowd grasped the situation and joined in the laugh, which continued until O'Donohue's Irish blood was up, and in a tone that I had never before noted, asked what the joke was, and where the fun came in. This started the crowd oft again, when one of the Roper troopers stepped into the breach with:

"All right, old chap, don't get your wool off. You see, we have no charge against these fellows, as we have not been able to catch them red-handed. They had been hanging round here for two or three days, so the camp fellows ran them out yesterday, with threats that if they showed up again they would get 'what for;' and now you quietly waltz the whole 'push' back again!"

There was danger, nevertheless, in O'Donohue's eye as he told the crowd to stand back. Then he asked the shanty keeper to give his prisoners a good supply of tucker at his own cost, and when that was done he ordered "The Ragged Thirteen" to right about face and marched them over two miles of the road we had just come. Here he took his farewell of them, warning them that as he had a good memory for faces, they had better refrain from troubling that part of the country again.

Although our performance was very like that of the good old Duke of York, who "marched his men to the top of the hill, and marched them down again," it nevertheless did a deal of good, and long after the laugh was forgotten, the pluck of O'Donohue was remembered[4].

Searcy's book was a popular read in 1912, but his detractors were many. In a later issue of the *Sunday Times* for example, an acquaintance of the Ragged Thirteen reviewed Searcy's work:

… Searcy's book may be interesting, but if his other

reminiscences are as truthful as that quoted, then the whole can be relegated to the 'Deadwood Dick' brand of literature; for a more unreliable, not to say cowardly, reference to some of the finest types of Australian bushmen of the early W.A. goldfields has never defiled the fair annals of journalism[5].

Unsurprisingly, twenty years after the events, the *Sunday Times'* own correspondent was not an accurate raconteur either, incorrectly claiming that Barney Lamond, and several others, were a part of the Thirteen. This writer claimed that the only 'depredation' the Thirteen had ever been involved in was "knocking over a bullock when the bags were low". This was forgivable, he or she thought, because "as any outbacker who possessed any semblance of backbone did the same in those days, it was not such a heinous offence"[6].

Anyway, Searcy's story was most unlikely, because *his* Thirteen – brilliant horsemen all – were on foot in his story; and *his* Thirteen had been run out by 'the crowd' at the Roper Bar Hotel, when, as a group, they were probably never there – the Roper Bar is too far east. The *Sunday Times* of 1912 agreed:

> ... The yarn about a swashbuckling John Hop arresting the whole bag will doubtless cause a contemptuous smile to lurk around the corners of the lips of the old greybeards who knew the Thirteen, for they (the 'Thirteen') were game enough to face a regiment of swaddies, much less a solitary trap. Fact of the matter is, Searcy, whoever he may be, has had to tax his thinking apparatus unduly in his efforts to conjure up any semblance of adventure in connection with W.A. in the eighties, and the effort was putrid[7].

If Alfred Searcy's books contained varying degrees of fiction, he also wrote of his adventures for the local newspapers, and the information in these articles seems more dependable. They record the places he actually visited, rather than romantically imagined. For instance, in 1889 he accompanied Hildebrand Stevens in the s.s. *Victoria*, (towing Charles Gore in the *Ark*), on a trip to the Victoria River Depot to deliver tonnes of stores for the cattle stations. His main interest then was the 1839 visits of John Lort Stokes in HMS

Figure 18: Victoria River Depot (Paul Foelsche, 1883, ph0111-0055).

Beagle, and the explorer Augustus Gregory's visit in 1857. Both these explorers carved messages into local baobab trees, and Searcy described what he saw eloquently.

At the Depot, Lindsay Crawford met the boats with a party of workers, and forty healthy horses, to collect the stores. Searcy reported that Crawford expected trouble on his return home through Jasper Gorge:

Mr. Crawford… says that the present season is the best he has experienced on the Victoria, although the rainfall had only been about 24 inches, it had spread over the whole season, in consequence of which, grass and water were in abundance. The cattle were looking splendid and had had a grand season. It was thought that the blacks would give some trouble this year, especially at Jasper Creek Gorge, about 50 miles above the depot, that spot being a favourite place for the blacks to meet and interfere with the teams. The gorge is several miles in length, and from its peculiar formation the blacks, if they had any sense, [they] would be masters of the situation, and could annihilate travellers by rolling rocks down the sides of the steep gorge[8].

The next year Searcy returned to Adelaide. He found it difficult to find paid work for a few years, but eventually took over his brother's job, as a clerk with the South Australian Parliament. He was considered an expert on Northern Territory affairs and consulted numerous times for his opinion. He may have wished to be remembered for his attempts to collar the Ragged Thirteen, but I could find no evidence to suggest he ever had anything to do with them.

By the 1920s, the Ragged Thirteen were half remembered legendary bushranger larrikins of the outback. Their story had been told and retold around so many campfires that the truth about them took a beating.

Occasionally, they appeared in short newspaper articles. One writer, for the *Truth*, met Thomas Nugent in 1907:

Travelling 30 miles south of Renner Springs, I came to the home of the CAPTAIN OF THE RAGGED THIRTEEN famous in 1885 [sic], for travelling overland from Queensland to Kimberley and sticking up all and sundry. The captain has now settled down as a squatter and is surrounded by a family of yellow picaninnies. In his sober moments he denies indignantly that he captained the ragged ones through their various exploits, but this writer saw him in his cups, when he openly boasted of the Thirteen's escapades, and bragged of sticking up homesteads for tucker and "borrowing" horses[9].

In the late 1920s there was a resurgence of interest in the

miscreants of the past. The *Gundagai Independent* remembered them in 1928:

> NOTORIOUS GANG. There were some smart drovers amongst the 'Ragged Thirteen' — a notorious gang of cattle duffers who slowly worked their way from Queensland to Kimberley. These men made raids on different stations along the route, usually at the end of the wet season, and ran off with a few hundred head of cattle from each property. They bred from branded horses and cattle and sold the young unbranded stock to some of the reformed cattle stealers who had acquired a piece of land and a registered brand. These men always camped some distance from their stock and worked them with aborigines, so that it was difficult to connect them with the stolen stock[10].

Their story was clearly a saleable item, so several journalists sought firsthand stories from old-timers to fill in the gaps. Chief among them was Ernestine Hill, who wrote for *Smith's Weekly*. In 1928, she wanted to know more:

> In the early '80's a number of filibusters crossed Central Australia from east to west. Some had undoubtedly "rustled" their mounts, others their outfits. When passing through settled country, they levied upon the flocks. They were known as the "Ragged Thirteen." Their objective was the Kimberley (W.A.) gold rush. Written history is silent about them. If any reader is able to supply authentic facts, will he please communicate with *Smith's Weekly* office in any of the Australian capitals. Their odyssey of travel deserves to be chronicled[11].

Ernestine Hill was a renowned journalist and raconteur who, despite being a single mother of a young boy, travelled widely. She spent so much time in the Territory and the Kimberley, that there is no doubt that she met those whom she claimed to meet and collected stories from them about others who were earlier pioneers. With trunks full of notes and biographies, she collated many of the stories of the north, and squeezed them into her 1951 opus, *The Territory*, which still sells today. In her book, and her articles about the Thirteen published in 1938 and 1939, the men were just "light-hearted scamps riding together, gentle grafters of the Great Unfenced, soldiers of outback fortune and in that hungry country, out for all they could get..."[12]. In a 1939 article, they were "Laughing Cavaliers of Gold". The only 'black mark' against them, Hill decided, was the theft of five hundred weight (230 kg) of horseshoes from Victoria River Downs Station.

Her major source was William Linklater (aka Billy Miller), the stockman who had worked for Tom Nugent at Banka Banka Station for several years. She claimed it had taken her seven years to gain Linklater's trust and interview him, though he was happy enough to publish his story himself in 1968.

Forgiven

The Thirteen had clearly found a place in Hill's heart. The romance of an earlier time was appealing, and she forgave them their transgressions of the law. She wasn't the only one. In 1933, the newspapers were clearly in a forgiving mood:

> Previous attempts made by isolated parties had met with disaster and death, but the determination of the Thirteen and the will to conquer all adversities pulled them through, and if they did steal stock and raid station stores, and shoot a few aboriginals in self-defence, they did so with but one purpose, that of keeping their lives intact in a country where the weak must fall[13].

Other writers were just as forgiving. Douglas Lockwood wrote of "carefree horsemen" led by Thomas Nugent in *Up The Track*, in 1964. To him, the Thirteen were "outback Robin Hoods, who took from the haves to give to the have-nots, generally themselves."

Lockwood was generous:

> ... If they wanted beef... well, there it was. If they wanted horses... well, why not? Let's take them. They were mounted bagmen, moonlighting throughout the outback in the days when communications, other than riders on fast horses, didn't exist. Anyway, they had the fastest horses[14].

Modern writers also show a degree of warmth towards the

Ragged Thirteen. To Stuart Traynor[15] they were a "gang of wannabe bushrangers" and a "motley bunch" who just "helped themselves to other peoples" property along the way, although "never at gunpoint".

Perhaps being "never at gunpoint" explains why the Thirteen barely rate as criminals. They stole hundreds of pounds worth of horses, cattle, horseshoes, food, and grog supplies, and they paid their bills, if ever, with dud cheques. But as they were never charged for their crimes, they got away with them, 'innocent until proven guilty'. To Barron, in his *Stories of Oz*, they were "Tea and Sugar Bushrangers", but this term, and words like 'larrikin,' 'vagabond', 'wannabe bushranger', and others, are words that somehow lessen their crimes.

Not The Ragged Thirteen

In our odd Australian way, where nineteenth century lawbreakers achieve cult status and become folk heroes – Ned Kelly is the prime example – it is easy to see why the Thirteen were elevated in the bushmen's stories to such status.

Australians love a good story of rogues, ruffians, and rascals, and they forgive many crimes if the yarns are good enough, and if they are not victims themselves. The Ragged Thirteen may have been surprised that they became so famous, and more surprised to find they were heroes:

> … Outlaws, horse-thieves, cattleduffers they may have been, but the name of the Ragged Thirteen has become a name of glory wherever bushmen outback talk of days gone by; their memory is revered, they've become heroes of the past, and the conquerors of a land that today still takes its toll of those who try to overcome its difficulties[16].

While the Thirteen still loomed large in people's memories, more than one group of charlatans jumped on their bandwagon. There were many who wanted to be like them, but they were always pale imitations. They fall into a group I call *Not the Ragged Thirteen*.

Journalists enjoyed writing about these wannabes. For example, this group ran amok in a Mudgee shearing shed in 1903:

> ... A disturbance occurred at Butterbone last Saturday, says the
> *Warren Herald*, but was fortunately quelled before anything of
> a serious nature took place. From what can be gleaned, when
> the roll was called, there were many more applicants present
> than required, and among those not engaged, were included
> what are commonly known as the 'Ragged 13' — a company
> of men who make a practice of visiting the various sheds
> during shearing season with the pretence of applying for work,
> but who invariably are the cause of mischief wherever they
> go. Sergeant Niles, who happened to be at the homestead, on
> being apprised of the trouble, soon put in an appearance and
> persuaded the men to leave, which they did... Assuming there
> would be no more annoyance, the Sergeant left for Warren,
> but on reaching his destination, word was received that the
> same men, with reinforcements, had returned and rushed the
> shearers' hut for 'tucker'. He instantly despatched Constables
> Pearce (Warren), and Greenwood (Nevertire), on whose
> arrival, the men left for good without further trouble[17].

Another wild mob went on a bender in Newcastle in 1924:

> ... Six members of a gang known as the "Ragged Thirteen"
> spent a hectic 10 minutes in the bar of the Great Britain
> Hotel, Newcastle, last Wednesday. They ordered drinks and
> refused to pay for them. They demanded money from other
> customers and punched them when it was refused. They then
> punched anybody who happened to be in the bar. Nellie, a
> barmaid, attempted to save one customer, and was nearly
> throttled. When Constable Stephenson appeared at the
> door, they rushed towards the second door. Here they met
> Constable Miller. At the third and last exit they encountered
> another constable. At the Newcastle Police Court, they were
> convicted and fined[18].

The editor of the *Toowoomba Chronicle* wasn't fooled. A little
maths suggested that these 'roughs' were not authentic:

> ... A crossheading in Tuesday week's *Chronicle* tells us of a
> gang of roughs, calling themselves 'The Ragged Thirteen,'
> taking possession of an hotel in Newcastle and playing
> up as only the depraved of our kind only can. They were
> masquerading. "The Ragged Thirteen" were in strong evidence

in the mid-eighties, and if any of their number escaped the gallows, he would be entitled to receive the old age pension. But judging from the swift manner in which they carried out, it is problematical if any of the crowd is on the Federal pension list[19].

This editor was right about age, but some in the media, for instance the writers for *Smith's Weekly* in 1928, wrote of a Queensland gang whose members chopped and changed:

The "Ragged Thirteen" were working their way overland to the Kimberley goldfield and made money en route by stealing cattle and horses and selling them as they went westward. It has been said that they never robbed a poor man and never refused to help a needy traveller. They often gave horses to weary and footsore swagmen and did not consider it a crime to duff cattle on a large scale from wealthy station owners. They made raids on many stations in West Queensland, and often cleared out with 200 or 300 head of cattle in one night. Leaving the Queensland border behind them and driving a large mob of cattle in front, the "Thirteen" eventually made their headquarters near Anthony's Lagoon. Here they bred from stolen beasts, then sold the young unbranded stock to new settlers on the Queensland side of the border. The band travelled with the stolen stock. These were sent ahead in the charge of aborigines, and if the police or irate squatters pursued them and came upon the stock, not a member of the 'Thirteen' was to be seen.

It was at Anthony's Lagoon that the gang had a disagreement and split up, some of the original members refusing to proceed toward Kimberley. Among these were Hanrahan and two others. They remained in the Territory, where they continued to steal cattle for several years. One of the trio settled on country west of Cloncurry, erected strong yards and put up a roughly constructed hotel. The locality was on the main route toward the Kimberley goldfield, and he did a roaring trade in his unlicensed shanty.

At the present time all that remains of the place are a few fence posts and half-a-dozen graves, the last resting places of foolish gold seekers, who may have tarried too long at the 'Orphan's'[20] shanty and drunk too liberally of the home-made grog. It was here that Hanrahan suggested they open a butcher's shop which would be well patronised by travellers. The hotelkeeper readily fell in with the idea, and, while he attended to the shop, Hanrahan stole the necessary cattle for the business from adjoining stations.

The business prospered and the man had no fear of arrest, as the nearest police station was 500 miles away. At last, the squatters expostulated so frequently that the cattle duffers offered to sell them their business for £1000.

The squatters refused, knowing only too well that they would only start a similar business perhaps 50 or 100 miles further along the road. At last, a posse of mounted police started out from Cloncurry, determined to arrest the duffers, but Hanrahan and his mate received word of their approach, fired the shanty and adjoining buildings, and disappeared.

Hanrahan joined up with another duffer and continued to steal cattle from Territory squatters.

Somewhere about 1892, during a disturbance in an aboriginal camp, Hanrahan was speared in the leg, and neglect of the wound left him with a stiff limb until the day of his death. The leg that would not bend at the knee prevented him from riding, and the cattle-duffing business knew him no more. The squatters in the Territory had good reason to thank the Myall black fellow who threw the barbed hardwood lance that ended Hanrahan's career as a duffer, for, if one believes his own statement, he was responsible for the theft of 8000 cattle in ten years. A few months before his death Hanrahan stated that, with the exception of himself, all the members of the "Ragged Thirteen" who left Queensland were dead. During the past twenty years he had been employed doing odd jobs on Northern Territory cattle stations, and as he was an excellent cook, his services were always in demand[21].

Several rural newspapers in New South Wales picked up the story of the death of Jack Hanrahan in 1929. Hanrahan was 58 years old in 1886, but nevertheless, in August 1929, it was reported that Jack was the last surviving member of the gang, and he had died on a Northern Territory cattle station aged ninety-one. Augustus Lucanus was sure that Hanrahan was a part of the gang:

Jack Hanrahan passed out on a Northern Territory cattle station the other day, at the age of 91. According to his own account he had "lifted" 8000 head in 10 years. He was a member of the "Ragged Thirteen," a collection of the biggest cattle thieves who ever levied tribute on the stations of Central Australia. Leaving Clermont in the early 80's, this band raided every station en route to Kimberley gold field in Westralia... Near Anthony's Lagoon, the main route to the gold fields, and 500 miles away from the nearest police station, the gang set up a pub and a butcher's shop, and fairly raked in the coin from travellers, who were fairly plentiful in those days[22].

This 'gangster' was dead after 35 years of living in an outstation with a stiff leg, a result of being speared "in a blacks' camp squabble"[23].

... Unable to ride, he had to give up cattle duffing, and settle down... He was the last survivor of the "Ragged Thirteen"[24].

Despite the real Ragged Thirteen being all much younger than fifty-eight in 1886, the story of one of them setting up a butcher's shop and selling the meat of locally caught duffers near Anthony's Lagoon appears now and then in the media of the twentieth century. The problem is that Anthony's Lagoon was a long way east of Abraham's Billabong, where the gang formed. It is possible that the Queenslanders in the gang were there at some time, because it was a stop on the road across the Barkly. However. those on the track from South Australia passed hundreds of kilometres to the west.

Hanrahan may have been the rogue butcher of Anthony's Lagoon, but he was not one of the Thirteen.

Another candidate for the role of rogue butcher was Jack 'The Orphan' Martin[25], whom Donald Swan recalled was:

... A gentleman who made an art of cattle stealing on a small scale was Jack Martin, alias *the Orphan*, one of the "Ragged Thirteen." Everyone who writes of the early Kimberleys mentions this crowd, and I am inclined to think they were not so black as they have been painted. The Orphan was a cool card. On his way over-land he got a notion to do a bit of butchering and sell the meat to the overlanders.

So, he camped about 100 yards from the road, built yards,

gallows, and meat shed, and started running in the squatters' cattle. The new business throve for six weeks or so, till the squatter got wind of the matter and rode up one day.

"Who's the owner of this establishment?" asks the station owner quite gravely. Quite as gravely, Jack admits that it is his. "Do you know whose cattle you're killing?"

"No, I don't, and I don't care a damn, either."

The squatter had a sense of humour and was a decent sort. Instead of getting wild, he said, "Don't you think you've had a fair spin here? How about moving on to the next run?"

"What? And leave my improvements?" cried the scandalised Orphan. "Not without compensation!"

However, the price he demanded was an absurdly high one, which was the ruination of his business, for the squatter set the police on him and he had to get for his liberty. This same Jack Martin, when mining at Ruby Creek later, set his tent afire one night when drunk and burnt one of his hands badly, losing the flesh right off it. Being crippled, however did not deter him from making a fortune at Coolgardie later, where he hit a good leader. He died only recently at Cue[26].

Jack Martin (aka Taylor) died in Cue, Western Australia of heart disease in 1918:

> ... Martin (otherwise known as Taylor), [was] one of the batch of prospectors known as the "Ragged Thirteen," who tramped from Kimberley to the Murchison goldfields in the early 1890s. The strong, stout heart which never failed in those days, at last gave way to the strain of years of hardship in the search for gold, and at 64 years ceased to carry on. Thus, another of the old prospectors of the prospecting days of Western Australia lies at rest on one of the fields where he laboured[27].

There were even more men who were said to be the "last of the Ragged Thirteen" to die over the next few decades. A poem published as *Back-to-the-Goldfields Ballad*[28] by the *Sunday Times* in Perth in 1938, refers to the Ragged Thirteen operating in the Kalgoorlie goldfields. None of the names of *this* Thirteen are familiar, but it is evidence that the romance of the gang appears to have continued:

…This is the rhyme of the Ragged Thirteen, a baker's dozen of braves

Who each lies cold in his lone costean[29], the best of Outback graves.

You can read this ballad in Appendix 1.

In 1939, the same paper discovered a man they claimed was one of the originals - but from him we hear even more unfamiliar names:

> … 'Camel Billy' Kirkwood is the last surviving member of the famous Ragged Thirteen, wild blades of the roaring 90's on the goldfields, and in the Kimberleys. "They were great, days, but they didn't last long enough," he said reminiscently yesterday as he sat in the casualty ward of the Perth Hospital waiting for the doctor's decision on the state of his eyes, which have been causing him trouble. He has lost the sight of one and is frightened for the other. Until he came down to Perth yesterday he was working on the Sturt Meadows station.
>
> *"Camel Billy they call me,"* he said proudly when asked his name. "They called me that at Kanowna years ago when I caught a bad-tempered camel for Paddy Whelan[30], you know, him that built the Shamrock Hotel in Perth. Yes, I'm the last surviving member of the Ragged Thirteen," he said. "If I'd stayed with them, I would have been dead, too. They used to drink a bottle of whisky a day. Let me see – there was Bill Cross, Tom McClay, Jim Jones, MacDonald, C. Burbride, and some others. Jones used to ride into a hotel bar on a colt and smash all the bottles on the shelves. On one occasion we got the Coolgardie express driver and guard drunk and drove the train to Perth ourselves. We tried the same thing on with a ship, but the captain put us in irons."
>
> Chuckling reminiscently under his bandages, 'Camel Billy' went off with firm step into the doctor. He will remain in Perth for further treatment[31].

A few weeks later, Mr N. Lewis wrote to the *West Australian* on behalf of the Western Australian Historical Society and told of a man who rode with the 'Ragged Thirteen' named Kyrwood. He may have misnamed Kirkwood, but other parts of his story agreed with the *Sunday Times* – some of it word for word. One comment in his letter suggests he may have interviewed Kyrwood personally: "He did not recall Tom Holmes"[32] he said, as if he had asked the question. Kirkwood was over 80 years old, but he would surely have remembered the leader if he'd been in the original gang during his twenties.

In 1944, The *World's News* reported, but did not name, the death of another 'last' of the Thirteen:

> ... The death was recently reported in Queensland of an old man reputed to be the last of the "Ragged Thirteen," the notorious band of bushmen which overlanded from Burketown (NWQ) to the Kimberleys in W.A. in the eighties. The Ragged Thirteen took by force anything they required on the overland trip, and as there were no police to worry them, they abided by the law of weight of numbers. Most of the band were wanted for horse-stealing and other offences, but on arriving at the Kimberleys they took new names and engaged in mining and pastoral work. Two of the band made good and acquired a large scope of country in the northwest of WA. and few, if any, of their neighbors [sic] knew of their past history[33].

In 1946, 'U.E.8', who must have known Billy Linklater, thought he or she would help the conversation along:

> ... 'U.E.8' writes: As there has been much controversy in different newspapers about who comprised the 'Ragged Thirteen' in 1866 [sic]. I am sending the names of those men. The names were sent to me by a friend of mine in the Northern Territory who knew a few of them. He also lived with Tom Holmes for two years at Banka Banka in 1901-2. Five of the men I knew very well, and the only survivor at the present time is Jack Daly. Here are the names – Tom Holmes, Sandy Murtle [sic], Jimmy Woodroffe, Jack Daly, Hugh Campbell, Wonaka [sic] Jack. Jim Carmody. Jim Fitzgerald, Jack Woods, Bill Smith, 'Jimmy the Rag,' Bob Anderson, and the thirteenth I think was George Brown, Wonaka Jack's brother[34].

The Australian press seemed to forget about the Thirteen after that, but tales of their escapades briefly faded into ghost stories. One was published by the *Western Mail* in 1953, and for readers who like a little extra, it is reproduced in Appendix 2.

In a long recount from 1933, the Ragged Thirteen terrorised western Queensland and morphed into a band called the 'Forties',

> In the early eighties there was a gang of men, headed by an elected leader, who had escaped from Brisbane, Sydney. Adelaide, and Melbourne, who were wanted by the police authorities in those cities. When they first formed up, they called themselves the Ragged Thirteen, but in after years, as their numbers increased, were known by the people of the district as the Forties, which name was most likely taken from Ali Baba and his forty thieves.
>
> The district in which they chiefly worked was a large scope of country between the Bulloo and Diamantina rivers, with Windorah and Jandali as the central townships. These men were a shockingly bad lot and would stop at nothing to gain their own ends; although I never heard of any of them committing actual murder, they were really a mild type of bushranger, and would ride up to a station and ask for anything they wanted, and, if not supplied, would quietly stick the place up and help themselves, whether it was money, rations, or fresh horses they wanted.
>
> One of their chief modes of livelihood was to invade the different towns at race meetings and rob men, either at card-playing or straight-out pocket-picking. Another thing I suspected them of was robbing Chinamen, who had been working on stations as gardeners, and putting them out of the way[35].

The events may have been real, but they were nothing to do with the Territory's Ragged Thirteen:

> Another brush I had with members of this gang took place… in Adavale… four of the Forties arrived in town and took possession of the Great Western Hotel and, having locked up the proprietor, his wife, and staff, proceeded to deal out free drinks to all and sundry. There were only two police in the town at that time, and as soon as they heard what had taken place, they called on four civilians in the Queen's name to help arrest the gangsters. The four called on were Dan Collins,

Gibson Stewart, Mick Bennett, and myself. The three former were armed with buggy-wheel spokes, myself, and the police with revolvers (I always carried one in those days).

We proceeded to the hotel, and as soon as we entered the bar, were greeted with a shower of bottles, which fortunately did little damage. Collins, who was a great athlete, bounded on to the bar counter and floored two of the Forties in two hits, and the other two men on seeing the revolvers put up their hands and surrendered.

Later on, they were brought to trial and received sentences of imprisonment in the Rockhampton gaol, and I heard that one of them, named Craig, died there as a result of the knock that Collins had given him[36].

In 1924, the following Ragged Thirteen tale had half of them locked up and the other half shooting up a Borroloola store:

The scum of four colonies, fugitives from justice, the gang had settled down and became the terror of the Roper and McArthur rivers, just inside the Northern Territory. They established their headquarters at Borroloola on the McArthur.

Two young Germans, who owned an adjoining run, were made the special prey of the marauders. They drove out the only butcher in the township at the point of the rifle and established their own shop. For supplies, four or five of the gang visited the Germans' station three times a week, slaughtered a couple of their bullocks and retailed the stolen meat to the inhabitants at six pence per pound. Two of the desperadoes, desirous of changing their place of abode—which was probably getting too warm for them, let McLeod, who kept the leading store in the township, in for about £600 by robbing him of cheques of the value of £300, and imposing upon him valueless cheques of the value of £300 more. McLeod started in pursuit of the robbers and swindlers, but lost his way, having perished from thirst. His body was found some days after, but the thieves hugged the sparsely populated portion of the Gulf country., were caught and sent to trial. McLeod made arrangements when leaving, for the storekeeper at McArthur station, John E. Cameron, an old Drayton schoolboy, to take charge of the store until his return. This Cameron did but struck trouble the first night. What remained of the gang came to the store to requisition goods "without money and without price." Cameron promptly refused to negotiate on those terms and a rush was made for the door, but Cameron acted promptly once again, and when the gang heard the bolt shot, they adjourned to their camp, and armed with rifles, returned to the store.

This building was not bullet-proof, being composed of packing cases. Calling upon the occupant to open the door, and receiving no reply, they began a lively fusillade. But they shot to kill; and blundered. Cameron curled himself in a corner under the counter, the bullets flew over him. Next morning the store was open for business as usual, and the gang paid spot cash.

This was in 1886, a couple of years after more of the gang were laid by the heels. But while they dominated the country on those two rivers, lawlessness reached its extreme limit...[37]

The real Ragged Thirteen now appear as a few lines in Territory history books and a couple of novels, but questions remain unanswered. I wondered if there is any trace of them left in the Northern Territory or Kimberley bush. Do the ringers on Victoria River Downs know the story? Is there any gold left in Halls Creek? Does the duffing of cleanskins still go on?

I could feel the need for a journey. If, as I believe, the Ragged Thirteen started their activities at Abraham's Billabong, just near the current day town of Mataranka, so too would I. How hard could it be to follow their 138-year-old trail?

Endnotes

1   *Northern Territory Times and Gazette*, 7 August 1886, Country Notes.

2   Barron's novel recounts how Donegan and Searcy tried to capture the gang by following them across the Territory to the Western Australian border – always one step too late. If anything like this happened, Searcy left the humiliation of their failure completely out of his own books.

3   For example: *Sunday Times*, 31 December 1911, page 4.

4   Searcy, 1912.

5   *Sunday Times*, 14 January 1912, page 18.

6   *Sunday Times*, 14 January 1912, page 18.

7   *Sunday Times*, 14 January 1912, page 18.

8   *Northern Territory Times and Gazette*, 4 May 1889, page 3. The comment about rolling rocks down from the hillsides set off a belief that this actually happened. Lewis (2021) and others have concluded that it did not. My own observations of the cliffs convince me that they are not the type of slopes where rolling rocks is even possible.

9   *Truth*, Brisbane, 1 September 1907, page 11.

10   *Gundagai Independent*, 13 September 1928, page 3.

11   *Smith's Weekly*, 27 October 1928, page 19.

12   Ernestine Hill, 1951, page 189.

13   *Uralla Times*, (N.S.W.) 23 February 1933, page 9.

14   Lockwood, 1964.

15   Traynor, 1016.

16   *Uralla Times* (N.S.W.) 23 February 1933, page 9.

17   *Mudgee Guardian* (N.S.W.), 8 October 1903, page 14.

18   *Daily Examiner* (Grafton, N.S.W.), 13 October 1924, page 2.

19   *Toowoomba Chronicle and Darling Downs Gazette*, 18 October 1924, page 13.

20   Jack Hanrahan may also have been called Jack Martin, otherwise known as 'The Orphan'.

21   *Smith's Weekly*, 22 June 1929, page 11. This paper employed Ernestine Hill, so she may be the author.

22   Augustus Lucanus, *Western Star and Roma Advertiser* (Qld.), Saturday 10 August 1929, page 7.

23   *Gundagai Independent*, 18 July 1929, page 3.

24   *Forbes Advocate*, 9 August 1929, page 3: Cattle Thieves 'The Ragged Thirteen'

25   According to Donald Swan, 'The Orphan' had been gaoled for five years in Queensland for sticking up Chinese on the road and robbing them (Lucanus, *Daily News* (Perth), 30 August 1929, page 6, *The Orphan*). Readers interested in Jack *The Orphan* Martin should also see *Northern Territory Times and Gazette*, 7 August 1886, page 2: McArthur and Roper River. Jack Martin and Jack Hanrahan may be one and the same – and known as 'The Orphan'.

26   Donald Swan (A. Pioneer) Kimberley Scenes, in *Western Mail* (Perth) 5 September 1929, page 9.

27 *Murchison Times and Day Dawn Gazette* (Cue, WA) 17 May 1918, page 2.

28 'Dryblower' *Sunday Times* (Perth), 21 August 1938, page 21.

29 A costean is a trench or small pit dug through surface soil or debris to the underlying rock to expose the outcrop of a mineral deposit.

30 Patrick Whelan was an 'identity' in Kalgoorlie and the eastern goldfields until his death in 1914. He did, indeed, build the Shamrock Hotel in Perth.

31 *Sunday Times* (Perth), 19 February 1939, page 6.

32 *The West Australian*, Fri 10 Mar 1939, Page 27: The Ragged Thirteen.

33 *World's News* (Sydney), 29 July 1944, page 18.

34 *Townsville Daily Bulletin* (Qld), 10 July 1946, page 5, Wonoka Jack.

35 'Ring Gidyea' *Sydney Mail*, 7 June 1933, page 13: The Ragged Thirteen.

36 'Ring Gidyea' *Sydney Mail*, 7 June 1933, page 13: The Ragged Thirteen.

37 *Toowoomba Chronicle and Darling Downs Gazette*, 18 October 1924, page 13.

Chapter 5
Travelling the Trail

By the early twentieth century, remote stations in the outback were occasionally serviced by visitors who would bring mail and supplies ordered from Darwin or Alice Springs. However, most Kimberley and Northern Territory bushmen also needed to use a 'mail-order'[1] system to buy goods from stores like Anthony Hordern and Sons, which was an early department store in Sydney. This company's emblem was the image of a Port Jackson fig tree that grew for more than one hundred years on Razorback Mountain, beside the Hume Highway near Camden in New South Wales. It was a marker my brothers and I used to look out for as we visited Sydney – especially since a nearby layby was a common place for Dad to pull over after his old FB Holden station-wagon boiled over, yet again. I remember the tree well but, unfortunately, it was poisoned in an act of vandalism in 1966[2].

In the early 1900s, this huge city-based store served many countryfolk well, including Tom Nugent. In 1907, he told the *Australian Star* that:

> ... "We send to Anthony Hordern's for clothing and boots,
> Yes! We send all that way, and I can tell you there is never a
> saddle strap missing: You see these boots I'm wearing; well,
> they cost me 6s 6d or 7s at Hordern's, but at our nearest store
> we'd have to pay 25s for them"[3].

I also needed boots before heading on my field trip to follow the Ragged Thirteen. If I had been in Port Darwin in the 1880s and 1890s, I could have wandered down to the corner of the Esplanade and

BOOTS! BOOTS! BOOTS!

MRS. A. KILIAN

BEGS to inform the inhabitants of Palmerston and up-country, that she has RECEIVED, by the "William M'Kinnon," a LARGE ASSORTMENT of Men's, Women's, and Children's BOOTS and SHOES, consisting of Men's Elastic Sides, Oxonians, Bluchers, Lace-ups (light and strong), Canvas Shoes, Men's Slippers, a superior class of Ladies' Kid and Patent Shoes, Children's Leather and Lasting Boots, also Babies' Patent Strap Shoes.

The ABOVE will be SOLD at about MELBOURNE PRICES.

PEERLESS GLOSS ALWAYS ON HAND.

Figure 19: Killian's Boots: *Northern Territory Times and Gazette*, 9 November 1878, page 1.

Smith Street and entered Charles Kilian's Boot Shop. Charles, or Mrs. Amy Kilian[4], could have sold me an elastic-sided pair from the range he imported "at *about* Melbourne Prices"!

If the Kilians had needed me to wait, I could have slipped down to Lot 419, opposite the construction site of the first two storey stone-walled hotel in Palmerston, later known as the Victoria Hotel, and into Samuel Brown's Coffee Palace for a brew and a game of billiards. I could even stay in one of their rooms, for 25 shillings a week. Both these places were flattened by the 'Great Hurricane' of 1897. A Chinese man was killed by debris whilst sheltering in the boot shop during the cyclone[5].

Nugent had used mail-order, and 120 years later I did too, before hitting the road to follow the Ragged Thirteen's trail. It was easier for me, of course. In 1921, Tom Cahill explained the problems of distance during his time at Wave Hill Station in 1886, to the *Sydney Morning Herald*:

> Our nearest mail station at that time was the Katherine Telegraph Station, which was 300 miles away to the north-east; while Hall's Creek, on the Kimberley goldfields, was an equal distance away In another direction. Sometimes the drovers brought our letters in, but when we wanted to send away mails we had to send men with packhorses, and it took them close on 12 days to cover the journey[6].

Online, I found some famous-brand boots from South Australia, for $649, through several bush supply stores. But I balked at the cost, and finally purchased an excellent pair of walking boots for $153 (plus $20 p&h). I then compared the price with the six shillings and six pennies that Nugent had paid. In today's dollars, according to the Reserve Bank's time currency converter, his boots cost him less than $60! Bugger!

Deciding against stealing a horse and pack animals, I serviced my ten-year-old Hilux, and readied for a journey that planned to emulate the track the Thirteen had taken in 1886 from Abraham's Billabong to Halls Creek. I also wanted to visit Nugent's Banka Banka Station and Arltunga, where MacDonald ran the Glencoe Hotel and where Woodford's remains lie in a lonely bush cemetery.

Instead of three hundred-weight of horseshoes and smithed nails, I packed a second spare wheel and a car fridge, but I reckoned that my swag, billy, and frypan were similar to those the Thirteen used. Getting into the 1880s theme, I included a slim volume of my favourite bush verse to recite or read around the campfire – a few drovers' tales would suit the mood, because joining me were my teenage sons, Harry and Roy. It was time, I thought, to inculcate them with an appreciation of life in the bush a century ago – albeit in an air-conditioned four-wheel-drive.

As it turned out, the route to the west was still flooded by the rains from a tropical cyclone named Megan. This storm had dropped vast amounts of rain as it crossed the Territory and the Kimberley, two weeks before, so the southern journey down the Stuart Highway was our only option. We would start with Banka Banka.

It took us ten hours to drive to the 142,000-hectare Banka Banka Station from Darwin. The Stuart Highway had suffered considerable damage from the recent rain, so the drive was slower than usual, but it is still a long way.

The buildings of Banka Banka Station that are open to the public sit just off the highway. For dozens of kilometres in each direction, signs advertise caravan and camping facilities and hot showers, so I was expecting that they would welcome all comers. I had emailed the address I had found on their webpage and, although I'd had no reply, I thought our arrival was at least expected.

Figure 20: Banka Banka Station's welcoming signs are spread for dozens of kilometres along the highway in each direction.

Three or four caravans were already comfortable in the van section of the park. Their occupants were busy cooking their dinners or watching their satellite TVs.

It was just after dark: to be precise, 7:10 pm. A bloke came out of his house to see us, a baseball cap pulled down low across his forehead. He was not smiling.

"Late," he said.

"We are hoping to camp here" I replied.

"But you're late. So late… we close at 5 o'clock, mate. We're not… it's dark already… late… late… I work 24/7 you know."

That apparently meant every hour except the current one.

"Well, I can't be the only person ever to turn up late… what do you usually do?" Long pause. By this time, I was expecting to have to hit the road again.

"You have a tent," he decided. "You can pitch it over there… $25 plus $5 late fee…". And that was it. I paid and he went back inside his house, I presume to brood, and we never saw him again.

Figure 21: Punkurr Punkurr Waterhole, Banka Banka.

Pitching a tent in the dark after a good rainy season in Central Australia is not always fun. Our torchlights brought in every winged insect within a hundred metres. Clouds of them swarmed around us, getting stuck in our hair, caught in our throats and eyes. Many of them were mosquitoes big enough to need a small shotgun to bring down, so, needless to say, we were zipped up and in the dark as quickly as possible.

Two kilometres from the camp is the picturesque waterhole named *Punkurr Punkurr*, nestled within a low range of rocky hills. We walked to it soon after dawn and found the secret hideaway of the mosquito army. We took a photo and quickly retreated. It must be a wonderful waterhole to visit during a drier season when the flying bloodsuckers were less numerous, but not this year.

This part of the Northern Territory is the traditional lands of the Warumungu and Warlmanpa people. The waterhole had been called *Punkurr Punkurr* by them for millennia, and when Tom Nugent leased the land in 1895 for his 1200 cattle, he retained the name in his mispronunciation of 'Banka Banka'.

Nugent wisely relied on Warumungu men as a workforce to help him run his cattle, and subsequent pastoralists have done the same. After Nugent died, the station was inherited by his sister and then managed by her sons, Nugent's nephews. They were three brothers named Ambrose. They built a homestead in the 1920s, just near where we had pitched out tents[7]. It is still there.

We went to have a look. It is a mudbrick and timber building with wide verandas on all sides. Restored in 2022, its eaves were so low along the verandas, I thought the Ambrose brothers must have been tiny, but when I bent double to pass under them, the cool air that met me quickly explained their design.

Visitors to Banka Banka

There was only one track across the middle of Australia, and every traveller used it to move overland from station to station. It followed the Overland Telegraph Line and Banka Banka Station was the first settlement north of the Tennant Creek Telegraph Station, so Nugent had numerous visitors. Some of them became famous after publishing books on their adventures. Jerome Murif was one. In 1897, he was the first to ride a bicycle from Adelaide to Darwin. Unfortunately, when he arrived at Banka Banka, Nugent was away:

> … reaching the cattle station (known as Bankabanka, I believe) there was no one at home except a few blackfellows and lubras, who greatly enjoyed the sight of a so ragged a whitefeller and the bicycle, but who were a very inoffensive lot of people[8].

A famous anthropological research trip, by Baldwin Spencer and Frank Gillen, travelled through the centre of Australia in 1901-2. Their diaries give more information about the lives of the remote cattlemen. Spencer recalled the day he spent with Nugent:

> … By 4 o'clock we had reached an outlying 'station' which consisted of two huts built beside a spring of water which the natives called Banka Banka.

> The owner & manager is a remarkable character & a splendid old bushman. His name is Thomas O'Brian Harrington Nugent, and he describes himself as the worst of the Harringtons, the last of the Nugents, and the King of Benaraban, which latter is the name of the station which

he once used to manage. His present abode, which is also dignified with the name of 'station,' is a hut about the size altogether of our dining room, built of logs between which the wind and dust & flies can enter freely. There is of course no floor except the earth and the furniture consists of one box, one short form, and a clean table.

The fowls wandered in and out at their own sweet will – dogs of course in plenty and now and then a stray pig. The walls are ornamented with pictures of prize fighters – 18 of them altogether – the only other individuals who are allowed to figure being Gladstone, Banjo Patterson, and a variety of Boer Leaders. The Bishop of Carpentaria spent a night here on his way down and was much edified.

Tom Holmes or Tom Nugent (you call him which you like) is a most interesting and picturesque man – a splendid type of the bushman. We had seen him before at Tennant's Creek when he had made Gillen's hair stand on end with wonderful accounts of snakes and great huge holes in the ground big enough to swallow buggy & horses and riders. He was astonished to learn that I had never heard of a certain Mr Richard K. Fox whose portrait occupied the place of honour in his gallery and most kindly presented me with a copy of the Police Gazette of New York of which remarkable paper he is the editor. That paper & now & again stray copies of the Bulletin comprise all the literature read by Mr Holmes.

Anyhow, we had a very interesting evening yarning about the Northern Territory where Holmes has lived – wandering over pretty well the whole of it during the last 35 or 40 years & amongst other things we had a real feast of eggs, which do not often fall to our lot here, so I ate 13 at one sitting[9].

The Bishop of Carpentaria, the Right Reverend Gilbert White, did indeed visit Banka Banka as Spencer recalled, and he too wrote the story of his travels[10]. Unfortunately, he did little else than describe the roughness of some of the gorges of the Ashburton Range on the station. Although, because he never mentioned the mosquitoes around the waterhole, his visit might have been more pleasant than ours.

Moving South

As a bonus, World War Two history buffs will be interested in the Heritage-listed Banka Banka Staging Camp, right across the highway from the homestead. This camp serviced the army convoys heading north to Darwin from Alice Springs. Travelling at 20 miles per hour and taking 11 days, these convoys needed a few of these staging camps along the Stuart Highway, and Banka Banka was the second.

Interesting as it is as a place to stop, the homestead and artefacts that remain are all from a time after Nugent had gone to Tennant's [sic] Creek Telegraph Station, on his final trip in 1911. So, not meeting anyone at the camp who knew anything of its history, we headed south and crossed Attack Creek, which was running with cool, clear water. Here John McDouall Stuart had turned around on his fifth attempt to cross the continent, after he was supposedly 'attacked' by 30 Warumungu tribesmen. They were angry that Stuart and his seventy horses had used up most of the water the tribe were relying on for survival. He recorded that:

> ... they seemed to be in a great fury, moving their boomerangs above their head, bawling at the top of their voices, and performing some sort of a dance. They were now joined by more of their tribe, so that in a few minutes their numbers had increased to upwards of thirty; every bush seemed to produce a man. Putting the horses on towards the creek, and placing ourselves between them and the natives, I told my men to get their guns ready, for I could see they were determined upon mischief. They paid no regard to all the signs of friendship I kept constantly making but were still gradually approaching nearer and nearer to us. I felt very unwilling to fire upon them, and still continued making signs of peace and friendship, but all to no purpose. Their leader, an old man, who was in advance, made signs with his boomerang, which we took as a signal for us to be off...[11]

We soon arrived at the Tennant Creek Telegraph Station. Nugent's last journey here, in 1911, ended in his death from 'dropsy'[12] and his grave lies just outside the station's fence.

The information boards at the telegraph station mention Nugent as a frequent visitor to the station when he was cattle herding at Banka Banka. The telegraph was, of course, everyone's major form of communication with the outside world. Pastoralists used it to track stock prices, to order in their yearly requirement of stores such as flour, tea, jam, sugar, and tobacco, as well as to keep in contact with friends and family. Maybe Nugent ordered his 6s 6d mail-order boots from here.

One information board says Nugent was the "clever and daring leader of the 'Ragged Thirteen,' a gang of vagabonds who roamed the Northern Territory and the Kimberley at the turn of the century [sic]." The choice of the word *vagabond* was interesting, and the only time the Thirteen have been described as such. I looked it up. A vagabond is "a person who wanders from place to place without a home or job". This term does not apply to the Ragged Thirteen. They were not 'aimless roamers,' but overlanders who were a part of a gold rush. 'Vagabonds' is a term that lessens their crimes of robbing cattle stations, as a gang... as bushrangers.

Nugent now lies in the tranquil surrounds of the telegraph station. In the end, he was a popular, and well-respected, pioneering cattleman.

Sandy Myrtle MacDonald and James Woodford also passed this way on their journey to Arltunga. This was before Nugent established Banka Banka – but possibly during the time he was working on the telegraph line and, though they left no record, of course they would naturally have caught up with old mates like Nugent if they were in the same area. After all, Tennant Creek Telegraph Station was the hub of social life for hundreds of kilometres.

But after that, they moved on to Arltunga, and so too, did I.

Arltunga

Arltunga was Central Australia's first town. Just over 100 km east of the Alice Springs Telegraph Station, the settlement predates the town of

Stuart (Alice Springs), declared in November 1888, by a few months. But it was a gold mining town, settled in a rush by hungry miners, so there was initially little rhyme or reason to its layout. However, eventually the central part was taken over by the government battery in 1898, and the post office and the assay offices were spaced along a main street nearby. Their ruins still exist, plus the old police station, and lockup, that sit on the other side of a small hill, a kilometre or so away. We followed the walking trail through them all, well netted against the flies.

The recent rains had transformed the East MacDonnell Ranges into a verdant paradise of thick grass. Unfortunately, the lush green pastures that we saw are nothing like those that MacDonald and Woodford experienced, because some areas are now a monoculture of buffel grass. This African grass (*Cenchrus ciliaris*) is an introduced perennial species brought in to feed cattle and stop dust storms by the CSIRO in the 1950s. Sadly, for the local plant populations, buffel grass can dominate and significantly damage natural ecosystems – including by increasing the risk of fire (large areas of the MacDonnell Ranges were scarred and denuded by fires in 2023). The old photographs of Arltunga show a bare landscape with almost no vegetation. The steam powered battery and everyone's cooking and warming fires used wood, and over the years, the miners needed to travel further and further out to collect it, but at least they didn't have to worry about grass fires.

Building materials, except stone, were rare and valuable, so most miners built their own houses by constructing low stone walls, cementing them together with mud and completing them with a canvas tent placed upon the walls[13]. Some had beautifully constructed flat-stone floors that are still in place, but the tents are long gone, of course.

The Arltunga ruins give us a fascinating glimpse of life in the White Range, a part of the East MacDonnell Ranges, more than a century ago, but several sites in the reserve particularly interested me,

Figure 22: A typical tent and stone accommodation in the Arltunga. This one was owned by J C Collison (SLSA, B-18346-3).

in regard to the members of the Ragged Thirteen. From whatever date MacDonald and Woodford arrived, the latter seems to have spent the rest of his life in the region. He scraped a living through fossicking – including collecting meteorites that found a ready market in Adelaide – and held jobs such as gaoler, minding prisoners in the watchhouses of both Arltunga and Alice Springs. He also held a store-keeper's licence in 1919, and earned money in any way he could, until his death in 1921. In 1920, a Commonwealth Public Works Committee visited Arltunga, and interviewed Woodford regarding the construction of the railway northwards from Oodnadatta. By then Arltunga was slowly dying – it was abandoned a decade or so later, but Woodford was still upbeat about its possibilities:

> James Woodford, prospector, who had been 42 years in the district, said the White Range was one of the best mineral propositions he knew of. The whole mountain carried gold, and it would pay to put it all through the battery. There were never any big companies at work at Arltunga, and the mining was not carried on in any systematic manner, through lack of proper ventilation, and on account of the presence of arsenical pyrites. Many miners had died of phthisis [tuberculosis], and the work on the field had ceased. In his opinion, it was impossible to successfully work the field unless a railway were constructed reasonably close. He advocated a direct route from

Figure 23: Arltunga police station and lockup now sit in a field of buffel grass.

Oodnadatta through White Range and the wolfram fields, all east of the telegraph lines[14].

The Arltunga police station and lockup where Woodford worked were built in 1912. They were renovated in 1985. It was a big job because their destruction had been hastened by the false rumour that gold had been hidden in their walls, and people had been active in their search for it.

According to Tom Leather, the Arltunga ranger we met as he was cutting the invasive buffel grass from the pathways, before the lockup was built prisoners were manacled to the police officer's bed, for safe keeping.

Luckily for him, Woodford's few months as a bushranger in 1886 were no impediment to working for the law in the new century. When I found his grave in the Crossroads Cemetery, this became especially apparent. Woodford's grave is one of only four or five marked graves in the cemetery and it is surrounded by a heavy stone wall and has a marble headstone. This is common in other graveyards, but Woodford's grave is the only fancy grave there. His headstone, and presumably the wall, were placed by his 'good mate' C.E. Cowle.

It didn't take me long to find out who Cowle was: Mounted Constable Charles Ernest Cowle was stationed at one or other of the Central Australian police stations for decades after 1899. He had also been a guide for the Horn Scientific Expedition in 1894, when the scientists explored Ayers Rock, Mount Olga, and Lake Amadeus to

Figure 24: Camel train at Arltunga c 1890 (LANT PRG280_1_1_374).

Figure 25: Woodford's Grave at the Crossroads Cemetery, Arltunga.

collect rare zoological specimens. Sir Baldwin Spencer was pleased with his service and noted that Cowle was "observant, cheerful and courageous, a great bushman with a wonderful knowledge of the country and the ways of the natives."

Woodford and Cowle must have been really good mates. The headstone is marble and was imported from Adelaide, where it was made by S.A. Monumental Works[15]. Freighted on the Ghan railway to Oodnadatta, it was, no doubt, then carried by camels the next 600 km. Its purchase was no small feat, and it was at no small cost.

Woodford was also respected enough to make *The Chronicle's* obituary columns:

> The sudden death occurred at Arltunga recently of Mr. James Woodford, a well-known prospector in the far north. He was 65 years of age and for some time has kept a store at Arltunga. He was noticed by Mrs. F. McGowan sitting in his [illegible] and as he was still there at a late hour the same evening, she went over to him and found that he was dead. In June last Mr Woodford gave evidence before the Federal Public Works Committee at Arltunga in favor [sic] of the direct route for the

Figure 26: Sandy MacDonald's Glencoe Hotel on the crossroads in Arltunga.

North-South line through the White Range and the wolfram fields to the east of the overland telegraph line[16].

The other major site I wanted to see in Arltunga stands next to the crossroads: MacDonald's Glencoe Hotel. Its ruins are small because much of the building was canvas or wattle and daub and only the stone walls still exist, but they include the kitchen and its chimney. MacDonald opened the hotel in 1910, at the age of 51, and may have then sold his store and slaughtering business and gave away

Figure 27: MacDonald was buried in the West Terrace Cemetery in Adelaide.

any pretence at mining. It was here that he lived out most of the rest of his life with his Aboriginal wife, Korulya, raising their daughter Myrtle. Eventually, nearing sixty, Sandy Myrtle MacDonald returned to Kent Town in South Australia to live with his sister, Annie, and he died in May 1919:

MACDONALD.-
On the 4th May, at the Private Hospital. Adelaide, Alexander (Sandy), of Arltunga, beloved brother of Angas Macdonald [sic], Prospect, and Mrs. Annie Tonkin, Kent Town, aged 60 years[17].

MacDonald was buried in the West Terrace Cemetery in Adelaide.

These days, of course, Arltunga is heritage listed and it is not permitted to camp there, but down the Binns Track is the Hale River Homestead, on Old Ambalindum Station. It was there that we headed for the night.

Ambalindum

Ambalindum is a huge station that covers more than 3,300 km² of the rugged East MacDonnell ranges. It was a thrill to visit because the country looked stunning in the late afternoon light. We passed a large number of bulls as we approached – the station's speciality – and entered a lovely cluster of houses and sheds that the hosts, Lynne and Sean Leigh, have developed for the tourist trade. Lynne explained that they'd just opened for the season, and we were her first customers. She encouraged us to camp on the lawns near one of the fire pits, have a beer in the bar, explore the old homestead, or walk the walking tracks that surround the homestead.

Exploration was a great idea. The bar/restaurant area and the old homestead are full to the brim with items the Leighs have collected at numerous stations they have managed over the years – old tools, telegraph insulators, signs, books, bottles – everything I could think of was there. In the old homestead's living room was a geological display – ores and mineral samples and even, to my amazement, a small collection of meteorites. I wondered if Leigh knew of James Woodford and his meteorite collecting 'business'. It was certainly a coincidence – and nice to know that space rocks still lie around this part of the country.

Lynne explained that Ambalindum Station had been settled around the beginning of last century by a pastoralist named George Cavenagh whose plan was to breed cattle for the meat trade he would easily win from Arltunga. Ambalindum was close, and the miners, or the storemen, would come through the hills, purchase the meat, and then sell it in the township. One of the reasons police were needed at Arltunga was because the cattlemen complained of losses – someone had been duffing their herds. I wondered who was responsible. I know of two blokes who had a history in that sort of thing… but that is just supposition.

Abraham's Billabong

Travellers on the north-south road continued to pass close by Abraham's Billabong until the Stuart Highway was constructed further west and the settlement of Mataranka was established in 1928. Bishop Gilbert White wrote in 1909 that he "passed Abraham's Billabong, a beautiful waterhole covered with lilies and surrounded by fine trees; then on four miles farther to Bitter Springs, where we camped". Nowadays, it is rare that anyone goes to the billabong, but

Bitter Springs is a managed reserve as part of Elsey National Park. It is a fabulous spot for modern-day tourists to lounge about in clear warm spring-fed waters, and it can become quite crowded during the busy tourist season.

We drove passed Mataranka on our return to Darwin after our Central Australian sojourn, without time to explore and look for the site of the wayside pub, and it was weeks before I could get back. When the roads soaked by Cyclone Megan at the end of the wet season were finally opened in May, I carefully planned my route with a couple of mates and set off on a quest to follow the gang across the Top End, starting from the billabong that, I believe, saw their genesis.

We camped near where the gang camped. Bitter Springs is now a major tourist destination managed as part of Elsey National Park[18]. The spring water stays at a constant 34°C, and travellers can swim for a hundred metres or more down a small river. Dozens of fresh-faced tourists can regularly be seen clinging to bright orange or pink 'noodle' floats slowly floating down their lazy river. Interactions with turtles, rainbow fish and archer fish are pleasant wildlife experiences for those with goggles, but the other scaly residents that might be expected there are gone. Rangers trap and remove any crocodiles they find in the waterholes before the park is opened for swimming in the early dry season. This far south, most crocodiles in these waters are the 'freshwater' species (*Crocodylus johnstoni*), but the proximity to the Roper and Waterhouse Rivers makes the arrival of the dangerous 'salt water' crocodiles (*C. porosis*) a possibility. Get bitten by one of them and your entire day is ruined.

It was here that cattlemen, and overlanders like the Ragged Thirteen, set up camp, often for extended periods while waiting for seasons to change. No doubt they modified the site and it looked very different to the managed environment we can see today. Gone is any evidence of horse yards or hitching rails, campfires or bark shade structures, that may have been here then. Not far away, there are concrete slabs that remain from a World War Two army camp and hospital. The springs have clearly been an important site for generations.

We followed the paved footpath that now weaves through a forest of large *Livistona rigida* palms[19]. The growing tip of these cabbage palms, as they are known, can be eaten, but the twenty-metre-tall monsters that I passed were blackened by fire, and the tops so high up that access to their edible tips was nigh impossible. Early settlers and explorers wrote of how they harvested the tips of young palms by the dozen. It became an important food source for them, as it has been for thousands of years to Aboriginal people. Removal of the growing tip unfortunately kills the plant.

The other dominant plants along the rivers here worth mentioning are the giant paperbark trees (*Melaleuca leucadendra*) and *Pandanas* (*P. aquaticus*) palms. The iconic paperbarks are huge and are an important part of traditional Indigenous economy. Aboriginal people used the thick papery bark for many things, but especially baskets, bedding, bandages, baby carriers, rafts, and shelter. Occasionally the trees can be a source of drinking water, if you find the right tree and know what to look for. I was grateful for the deep shade they cast on a hot day.

The multi-stemmed *Pandanas* plants hug all the creeks and rivers of the Top End. They have long sword-like leaves that are edged with tiny thorns, and prop roots in the water that are important nurseries for fish and other aquatic animals. There may be eleven or more species of *Pandanas* in the Territory and they are an important plant for Aboriginal communities. Baskets, fishnets, canoe sails and other items are made from their leaves, and rafts from their stems. As an added bonus, their seeds are edible, though very difficult to extract from their hard woody fruits.

We were soon to experience the unpleasant nature of *Pandanas* leaves.

The warm water from Bitter Springs flows into the Little Roper River, and our destination was a further two kilometres upstream of

Figure 28: The beautiful Abraham's Billabong.

this stream. I had no idea what to expect of the billabong, except that from aerial photographs and maps, it looked like a small body of water, a few hundred metres long, surrounded by thick forest. Patches of sand were visible on the photographs, along the water course towards Bitter Springs, so I hoped the best way to get there would be to just follow the riverbed. Unfortunately, this early in the dry season meant we were soon not only crossing a swamp, but one where the water was mostly hidden by piles of fallen pandanas leaves. These crunched loudly underfoot, and their sharp thorns needed to be avoided, but scratches soon appeared on my legs and tiny rivulets of blood trickled into my socks.

The Little Roper River here is made up of many tiny streams that squeeze through the *Melaleuca* and *Pandanus*. Huge golden-orb weaver spiders swing, spread-eagled, across the middle of their extensive webs. The giant females are tendered by tiny males, who must live their lives in a wary co-existence to avoid being a meal themselves. Several times we skirted around webs that were too thick and low to duck under.

An immature nankeen night heron watched us pass without fear. Relying on its mottled camouflage plumage, it allowed me to within a metre with my camera before edging away. We crossed a small stream via conveniently-spread tree root steps that split the creek into small rapids and soon found ourselves on a low sandy beach with our first views of the billabong. I could see high ground on the eastern shore, so waded barefoot and alone across another stream and pushed through the thick undergrowth for a hundred metres or so before I could sit in the shade and rest on the soft trunk of a *Melaleuca* growing at an angle out across the water.

Stretching before me was a typical Top End wild billabong. The words 'iconic' and 'magnificent' came to mind because Abraham's Billabong is simply stunning. It is a broad stretch of deep water, longer than I could see from my vantage as it curved away in the distance. Egrets and herons were obvious residents, and I could hear, and faintly smell, a colony of flying foxes nearby.

The high ground behind me was probably the only place suitable for the building of a country store. A quick scout around showed nothing but dense bush. Nevertheless, my sense of the historical events that occurred near here was almost palpable, heightened by my isolation. Mat Kirwin's country store and pub were long gone, but I felt the echoes of the drunks at the bar, their laughter and their noisy fights, and the whinnying of their horses waiting patiently for cattlemen to finish their partying. This was where the Ragged Thirteen became a gang, albeit an ephemeral one, that clung together out of mateship for just a few months.

A small crocodile swam across the surface about fifty metres away. I assumed it would be a freshwater crocodile, a fish-eater, who would pose no danger to me if I chose to swim – but too long in the Top End makes me wary of waterholes like this. Large saltwater crocodiles can walk tens of kilometres across country in a good wet season, and the nearby big rivers were closer than that.

Figure 29: Katherine Sportsman Hotel and Gallon Store.

So, I left the billabong in peace. Its birds and reptiles, fish and unseen mammals are still doing whatever it was they were up to on that day. I felt that no one had been there for a long time, and maybe no one has been there since, though that is most unlikely, because Mataranka town is just a few kilometres away.

Early the next morning we arrived in Katherine. The Hilux was refuelled, and a quick stop in the little mall on the main street allowed me to buy a blanket, needed because the night had proved colder than I had been expecting.

Surprisingly, there are some remnants of the old town as the Thirteen would have seen it a little upriver.

The Sportsman Hotel and Gallon Store was built on the banks of the Katherine River in 1887, by Bernard Murphy. This was a few months after the gang was there, but it is contemporary enough to give an idea of how most buildings in that era were constructed in the Territory. Milled timber and corrugated iron constructions, like this, are prone to wood rot, termites, rust, and fire, so this remnant is precious indeed. Trading until 1948, the original licence was for the 'Sportsman Hotel and Pioneer Cash Store', a name it retained until 1915, when it became known as the Gallon Licence Store. One gallon was the *minimum* amount of alcohol it was permitted to buy under a 1915 liquor law. Maximum was a dozen quart bottles or two dozen pint bottles, and they were supposed to be taken away by one person, and not drunk on the premises. The picturesque banks of the Katherine River, about a hundred metres away, must have seen some lively parties.

The store was open during World War Two until the Japanese bombed the town on 22 March 1942. During this raid, a bomb fell a few metres away, killing an Aboriginal man named Roger, and severing a fingertip from a man named Noel Hall. The bomb crater is still there, protected by a broken fence and a painted sign made from an old circular sawblade, lying flat on the ground.

Jasper Gorge and the Victoria River Depot

Leaving Katherine, the route southwest is now the Victoria Highway. The Thirteen would have ridden this way, following the tracks of the stock route, and they then would have passed through Delamere Station, further south. Today, this is reached by the Buntine Highway that joins the Victoria Highway and Top Springs. Delamere Station is now under military control, and soldiers practise firing missiles there, so it was not a place we would be welcome to wander around. Instead, we took a longer, and more interesting, route to VRD, that passed through the narrow Jasper Gorge. The Thirteen probably never used this route, but others did, and it was an important part of the Victoria River Downs story. We would join the Buntine Highway at Top Springs after a visit to VRD.

The Jasper Range was named by the explorer, Augustus Gregory, in 1856. The rocks of the range turn an impressive blood red, the colour of jasper, at sunset. The gorge and its creek took their names from the range. Jasper Creek leaves permanent waterholes as it flows through the gorge, even in the driest of seasons. The area has therefore always been important to the local Ngarliwurru people, who believe that the gorge was created by Walujapi, the black-headed python, during the Dreaming, when the great curving walls of the gorge were pushed up to fifty metres high by the snake, as she travelled through. Other Dreaming sites also exist there – Mulukurr the 'devil dog', Wurliyinki the red ant, and Wanujunki, a turtle Dreaming site in the shape of a single huge boulder.

After Gregory and his party had gone from the area, white men left it alone for the next thirty years. Then, in 1884, Lindsay Crawford found that he could travel the full length of the gorge, from the plains of the south, where he was establishing VRD Station on behalf of Charles Fisher and Maurice Lyons, to a supply depot he would build on the Victoria River.

Jasper Gorge soon became an important shortcut to VRD and Wave Hill Station workers bringing stores down from the Victoria River Depot. In the early days there was "just sufficient room between precipitous walls of red sandstone for a road to be forced through"[20]. But it was not good enough, so in 1886, a contract was given to Charles Gore for the construction of a road through the roughest part of the gorge. Boulders, that were too big to push aside, were destroyed by dynamite, the noise from which must have been quite alarming to the local Ngarliwurru people. Wanujunki, the turtle Dreaming, was one that unfortunately rested right in the path of the road makers.

Suddenly, there was resistance to the invaders. Charles Gore and his team were surrounded by many warriors, some of their horses were speared, and they had no choice, but to hunker down in their camp. Then:

> … on the third day… at about 3 in the morning the blacks tried to rush the camp. I jumped up and crawled from under the dray, and waking up all hands told them to watch me, and if I fired to all fire in the same direction. Almost immediately the horses began to snort and rush about the yard, so I fired, and all hands also emptied their revolvers. We heard a rush

through the scrub towards the range, the dog following, and although we were not troubled any more until daylight there, was no more sleep that night…[21]

They were harassed for several more days, but eventually Lindsay Crawford arrived with reinforcements. With an armed guard, Gore was able to complete his work.

Today, the Buchanan Highway through the gorge is well-made and, being recently graded, posed no problems. Just east of the narrowest part of the gorge is a picnic spot on the creek, and we stopped for lunch in the shade of two large ironwood trees.

Cattle were once driven through here on their way to market. In 1885, Donald Swan and Bob Button were the first to bring a herd through the gorge. Following Crawford's route, they were surprised to be greeted by Aboriginal men shouting, "Good day, good day!" from the cliff tops. They were not always so friendly. Ten years later there was an attack on two men who were carting stores to VRD through the gorge from the Victoria River Depot. John Mulligan and George Ligar were both wounded but they escaped, leaving their wagons to the attackers.

As we ate lunch, I read aloud the story of the attack as it appeared in the *Times* in 1895.

… between 8 and 9 o'clock, Ligar states that he was surprised by feeling a spear strike him in the back. He sprang up and was in the act of going for his rifle, which was hanging on the near side of the wagon, when he was struck by another spear in the face. At the same time Mulligan called out that he was speared also.

Mulligan, who was speared in the thigh, succeeded in extracting the weapon, and then commenced firing shots from his revolver. By this time Ligar had found his rifle, but to his disgust it would not work, and the blood from the wound in his face running all over and about it made the task of rectifying it in the darkness a hopeless one, but being handed a revolver by Mulligan, he fired three or four shots at random.

… During the day Ligar got down enough bags of flour, sugar,

Figure 30: Two horse drays with stores for VRD Station and the supply launch *Victoria*, at the Victoria River Depot (Paul Foelsche, 1893, SLSA B-5053).

Figure 31: Jasper Creek as it heads into Jasper Gorge. The Buchanan Highway is now an easy drive through.

&c., to form a barricade round the wagon, Mulligan, who was unable to move, keeping guard with both the rifles and doing good service in keeping the blacks at bay. Having completed their barricade, and having two good watch dogs, the two men camped that night in comparative safety and comfort. On the morning following, a large band of blacks and gins made their appearance but took good care not to expose themselves more than possible. Mulligan endeavoured to parley with them, but Harry, one of his own boys, cut this short by saying.

"We will kill both you white b--s tonight."[22]

They were dreadfully wounded; the spear had penetrated Ligar's lung, and he "became alarmed on finding his breath escaping through the aperture". And Mulligan was in such pain from the spear in his leg that he could not walk. After several days, the pair managed to catch two horses and rode them back to the Depot, but finding no one there, had to go a further 40 kilometres, to Auvergne Station.

They eventually made it to Darwin Hospital and recovered under the care of Doctor O'Flaherty and the nurses[23]. They were lucky, but the reasons for the attack remain obscure. Mulligan had carted stores through the gorge for nine years beforehand and had employed many of the local Ngarliwurru men to help get his wagons through[24], paying them with sugar, tea, flour, and tobacco – the currency of the time. Many Ngarliwurru knew Mulligan's name, and other travellers through the gorge would hear it being called[25]. The real reasons for the attack are lost in time and can only now be guessed at. The worst part of the story is what came next.

Jack Watson, then the manager of VRD, was outraged. He gathered a posse of seventeen white men and went on a killing spree. Together, they killed sixty or more people at a place named Kanjamala, about 20 km from Jasper Gorge. Few locals will visit this place, even now, because of this massacre[26].

Watson captured three women on this expedition. One had a broken arm, another had been whipped, and the third was lactating – although she no longer had a child with her.

Watson died in 1896, no doubt to the relief of many in the tribes of the north. He was either drowned or taken by a crocodile, or both, in the Katherine River[27]. He was last seen by his mate, George Ligar, holding onto a log during a swim across the river wearing a distinctive straw hat. Neither his body, nor his hat, were ever found. While few ever speak ill of the dead, especially in obituaries, Watson's obituary was long, complimentary, and unfathomably forgiving:

> ... the deceased, in his associations with other men, was a thorough 'rough diamond' – painfully wild at times, but never wanting in generosity, kindliness of heart, and bravery, three manly attributes which, to use an old quotation 'cover a multitude of sins'[28].

These attacks and the subsequent massacres had occurred not far from where we were eating lunch. We packed up our lunch things in silence, each with their own thoughts, and got back on the road. A truck passed by, but no one else was seen during the whole time we were in the gorge. It was the same in the following 60 km to VRD Homestead. The Buchanan Highway runs from near Timber Creek, through VRD and Top Springs, and across the Murranji to the Stuart Highway but, at least early in the dry season, it is little used.

Victoria River Downs

Victoria River Downs is the most iconic cattle station of Northern Australia. VRD is currently owned by the Heytesbury Pastoral Company and as noted elsewhere, it was once the world's largest pastoral lease, with an area of 41,000 km². Nowadays, much of the former station is Judbarra/Gregory National Park, and the current station spreads over about 8,900 km². It runs nearly 100,000 head of cattle over four separate stations – VRD, Moolooloo, Pigeonhole, and Mount Sanford, with Humbert River Station as an out-station to VRD. Rusty Richter is the general manager of them all, with the individual sections run separately. Julie Richter is the manager of the VRD section. I had been in contact with Julie over several weeks, telling her that we were interested in visiting to chase up any history of the Ragged Thirteen that was possible to find. All I could offer her was their story, but it seemed enough, and with traditional country hospitality, we were warmly welcomed to the station, loaned the guest house for accommodation, and fed in the camp kitchen with the staff.

The VRD homestead is built on the high bank above the Wickham River. It is actually a small village, with several homes, work sheds, a generator shed, and a recreation club building, that together sit around a 'common' of green grass, with numerous shady trees. Our first view of the village was across the airstrip from the gates. Signs warned us to drive at 10 km per hour on the dirt tracks through the village. This made sense when we saw the helicopters parked just to the left of the gates. They must have a perennial dust problem.

Julie welcomed us on arrival and talked of the history of the station buildings around us. Some had been second hand purchases, translocated from Katherine, others were built in the 1980s. Unfortunately for me, chasing nineteenth century villains, there is nothing here from that time. The Wickham River site was chosen in the 1890s because it was on high ground, and thereby flood proof. Also, being on the northern side of the river, it is accessible to the road through Jasper Gorge and the Victoria River Depot[29]. The original camp, built by Lindsay Crawford, is actually at least 40 km further south on the Pigeonhole road. It is one of two possible locations, as two were 'settled' at the same time, at Stockyard Creek and Gordon Creek. The Stockyard Creek homestead was originally called Fagin's Camp, but its name was changed later to Pigeonhole[30]. Gordon Creek is more likely to have been the head station. Hildebrand Stevens described it in 1891:

> … Hip roofed house 30' x 20' Iron roof paper [bark] walls.
> 10 ft verandah. Good Kitchen. One Building including Beef
> room, Saddle room, Men's room 50' x 12' all papers. Small
> Blacksmith's shop lean-to, bellows etc. Complete. 1 set Cattle
> yards. Capable of working 1500 head of Cattle. 1 Sq mile
> paddock[31].

Figure 32: Victoria River Downs.

Unfortunately for me, both these sites were unreachable. Due to the height of the water at the crossing of the Wickham River, the access road was still cut. Nevertheless, there were things to see at the modern homestead and Julie directed us to the ruins of a two-storey building that she called "the old hospital". It was on the riverbank about a kilometre away. She also suggested we visit the VRD Cemetery.

The building was a hospital built by the Australian Inland Mission in 1923. It was called Wimmera House and, despite now being abandoned, it remains an attractive old wooden framed structure with corrugated iron walls and roof. It has views overlooking the Wickham River. Judging by the high bar on the first floor (complete with a footrest for the drinkers), the building's last incarnation was as a recreation club that catered for a different kind of health.

The most exciting part of the visit for me was the large olive python curled up in the downstairs fireplace. Crouching down to photograph it, I backed off after it struck out at me several times and

Figure 33: The Olive Python in Wimmera House.

Figure 34: Wimmera House, an Australian Inland Mission Hospital, on the banks of Wickham River, VRD, was not immune to flooding (Ellen Kettle, 1955, LANT, ph0127-0409).

lay poised for another. I had no desire to be bitten by a three-metre python.

The VRD Cemetery holds the graves of several dozens of the station's pioneers, dating back, as far as I could tell, to 1910, though several early graves were unmarked and undated. Sadly, there were several babies' graves, but more often, the occupants of the cemetery were a "long time stockman and valued station worker of Victoria River Downs", ex-soldiers, or fondly remembered mates.

One 1927 headstone belongs to the then owner of Humbert River Station, William Julius Schultz, and his brother Albert Frank Schultz who were "two of Queensland's best horse and cattle men". William was "accidentally killed while riding a quiet horse and striking his head against a tree through the horse shieing [sic] and the saddle rolling with a loose girth"[32]. He died in the hospital building we had just visited. Albert had a more conventional death, dying either of appendicitis (headstone) or fever (obituary), aged 42, in 1925[33].

Another in the cemetery is Tom Graham, the station manager between 1919 and 1926. Graham famously started the VRD Races, a two-day competition for which cattlemen would ride "500 miles to attend". His obituary says that he "was known as an exceptionally active and capable stockman, and continued in active work right to the end, although he must have been quite 70 years of age"[34]. Gus Anderson also lays there. He was a Norwegian all-rounder who arrived in 1910, and remained there until his death by suicide, on Boxing Day, forty-six years later[35].

The next morning, before hitting the road again, we called into the VRD Social Club because it displays photographs of the station's history and bits and pieces of station equipment that were worth a look at.

But we were soon once again on the Ragged Thirteen's trail, heading southeast, on the Buchanan Highway, to meet the Buntine Highway at Top Springs, and from there to the west and Halls Creek.

We crossed several small creeks and rivers still with water in them, but they were nothing compared to the magnificent Victoria River at the Dashwood Crossing. Its waters were flowing fast, and the 100-metre crossing was as deep as the wheels of my Hilux. The high banks on both sides were covered with a fine layer of silt, showing that in its full flow, just weeks before, the river was at least ten metres deeper. Rusty Richter, and his team from VRD, had already cleaned

Figure 35: The VRD Cemetery.

Figure 36: The Dashwood Crossing of the Victoria River.

up the sand and mud from the crossing and fixed some of the worst patches of wet season damage along the highway, so travel through to Top Springs was quick and easy.

Top Springs

Top Springs is a hotel and roadhouse at the crossroads of the Buchanan and Buntine Highways. It was undeveloped bushland in 1886, when the Ragged Thirteen passed by, of course, but we stopped there for fuel (at $2.80 per litre) and pondered its more recent history.

Top Springs was declared a town in 1976, but it is still little more than the roadhouse known as The Wanda Inn. In the 2016 census, the town boasted a population of three, and I suspect little has changed since. When we arrived, a maintenance man was doubling up the locks on the front door. He said that the alcohol they sell is a target for local miscreants from nearby outstations, and break-in attempts are quite common. A young Irish woman, who was travelling the country on a working holiday, sold us fuel. Neither of these Top Springs residents knew anything about the history of the place, or the scandals that followed its original owner, Thelma Hawkes.

In 2022, Melbourne-based author Jon Faine[36] authored the incredible story of this woman, known to everyone as 'Ma' Hawkes, or more disparagingly as "Old Leather Tits". Her life there as a ruthless publican and store owner makes for a fascinating read. After Thelma and her husband, Sid, parted ways, Ma lived alone at Top Springs, for decades, charging an arm and a leg for the grog she sold, and squirrelling away her earnings in a biscuit tin. She died of an asthma attack in 1981, and it was then that the real scandal started. The attending policeman, 24-year-old Constable Kevin Dailly, who was stationed at Wave Hill [Kalkarindji] Police Station, discovered a huge pile of cash hidden in her upstairs house and helped himself to about $28,000. With nowhere to go, he buried his loot in the station yard at Wave Hill, in a plastic bag, planning to use it to buy a car in Darwin, the next time he was there. He would have got away with it too, if it had not been for Len, his excitable pup, who chased a frog a few weeks later through the yard. In full view of the station gardener and a Senior Constable, Len was digging after the frog and suddenly spreading dollar bills around the yard. The truth came out, and Dailly was locked up for six months. He was 106 years too late to join the Ragged Thirteen.

Knowing this history, we were interested to get the lay of the land – which didn't take long. Ma Hawkes lived in an upstairs flat in a building behind the roadhouse, and we walked around its outside. It was shut up tightly and looking decidedly derelict. Perhaps no one has lived there in the 40 years since Ma died.

The Buntine Highway

There are 400 kilometres of highway from Top Springs to the Western Australian border. Roads to various cattle stations lead off on both the north and south sides of the road, but the only town on the route is Kalkarindji. The country is mostly flat the whole way, and often almost treeless, with grassy plains stretching further than we could see. It is beautiful cattle country, I thought, and no wonder Augustus

Figure 37: The Wanda Inn, Top Springs, at the junction of the Buchanan and Buntine Highways.

Gregory was impressed. We saw emus, bustards, wedge-tailed eagles, a myriad of small birds, black-headed pythons, and other snakes crossing the road. Three brolgas waded in the shallow water of one of the creeks.

The highway is single-laned and sealed as far as the community of Kalkarindji, and graded dirt from there to the west. We stopped at the community's shop for a coffee break and an early lunch.

Kalkarindji used to be known as the 'Wave Hill Aboriginal Township,' and its land was once part of the Wave Hill Cattle Station, whose headquarters are not far from the community. Why it is no longer a part of the station is an important part of Australian history. A group of Aboriginal station workers made this place famous in 1966, and they are still revered as the founders of the Land Rights Movement across the whole continent. It was here that Vincent Lingiari led the Gurindji strike, and the 'Wave Hill Walk-Off', to protest against oppressive labour practices and land dispossession. Their protest lasted nine years and eventually led to the Aboriginal Land Rights (Northern Territory) Act of 1976, and that, at last, allowed for groups of Aboriginal people in the Northern Territory to be granted title to their traditional lands. A famous photo of Prime Minister Gough Whitlam, pouring sand from his hand into Lingiari's on 16 August 1975, became a symbol of the movement. There is a magnificent mural of the photo, painted on a wall in Bennett Street in Darwin, and numerous songs and books have been written about the strike[37].

Like VRD, Wave Hill Station has an early history. The original cattlemen who established the station were Nat 'Bluey' Buchanan and Sam 'Greenhide' Croker, in 1883. Buchanan had read a description of the country in Augustus Gregory's journal and based on that, and lifelong experience in the bush, he leased a thirty square mile section of country that he had never seen. Sam Croker brought in the first mob of cattle, and they were followed by 3,000 more, delivered by Tommy Cahill in 1884 and 1886. Distance meant that getting cattle to market was a major problem, but the Halls Creek gold rush was a boon to Wave Hill, just as it was to VRD and the other early stations.

Cahill was interviewed in 1921:

… In 1885 gold was found at Kimberley, and in 1887, Mr. Gordon and I took 200 head of fat cattle up to the goldfields. We made a show of boughs, in which Sam Crocker [sic] slaughtered the cattle. We also cut down a gum tree, from which we made a butcher's block. We then sold the meat in a rough and ready fashion to the miners. Sam Crocker went to Wave Hill in 1883. He was afterwards murdered by a half-caste at Auvergne Station[38], on the Victoria River.[39]

Leaving Kalkarindji, we crossed the Victoria River once more and headed west across Mitchell grass plains that groaned under the weight of the grass that had followed the recent wet season. The dirt road was recently graded, and if anything, was in better condition than the sealed section we had just been on. As the kilometres rolled by, we crossed stations that remain only names to me: Limbunya, Inverway, Bunda, Kirkimbie, and in Western Australia; Nicholson, Flora Valley, Leedawooloo; each with its own history. Many were on the original stock routes to the Kimberley.

The Ragged Thirteen crossed this country laden with the goods they had stolen from VRD. It would have taken them a few weeks, but because the road was so good, we were in Western Australia within hours. The Buntine Highway ends, just inside the border at Nicholson, and joins the Duncan Road in its track south from the Victoria Highway to Halls Creek.

The first cattle station settled in the East Kimberley was the Ord River Station. In 1886, it was managed by Bob Button[40] who, as has been mentioned, helped Buchanan establish the station on behalf of graziers W.H. Osmand and J.A. Panton of Melbourne, in 1884, and stayed on as its manager. He also actively explored the area between Derby and Cambridge Gulf, and Buttons Crossing and Buttons Gap are named after him.

Charles Gaunt was in awe of Button's bushcraft skills. "Bob

Button," he wrote:

> … was a great bushman, forming the Ord River Station.
> Button used to singlehanded, no black boys, take horses and
> go out for weeks exploring the country for miles. He knew the
> Ord River district like a book. Later he died in Hall's Creek.
> Truly a great bushman. In those days there were no roads for
> hundreds of miles and blacks were numerous[41].

The Duncan Road through to Halls Creek passes well south of Ord River Station. As it travels around the East Kimberley region in tectonic terms, it almost marks the line where the Kimberley craton collided with the North Australian craton during the Proterozoic era, over a billion years ago. We entered what geologists call the 'Hooper and Lamboo Complexes' and the Halls Creek orogeny. All this means is that this area was the site of massive geological convergence and mountain building, sediment formation, twisting and folding of land masses, and volcanoes, over hundreds of millions of years. This is why it is so interesting to geologists. The Halls Creek gold rush owed its genesis to this tectonic activity. So too, did the Argyle diamond mine to its north, and all the other mines in the area that dig up everything from iron ore to the rare earth mineral, dysprosium.

We were no longer on vast flat plains. The road skirted around and crossed low mountain ranges and several rivers between them, and we eventually reached Sawpit Gorge, our camp for the night. Wow! Two days on the plains hardly prepared us for the rugged beauty of this place.

The creek was still running, and the gorge was full of water, and fish, turtles, Merton's water monitors, and a whole range of birds enjoyed its depths and the forested banks of the creek. On each side, cliffs rose more than thirty metres, and it was stunning. We camped on a sandy beach under a full moon, our firelight flicking on the gorge walls, and yarned the night away, aware that the Ragged Thirteen were never this far south because they followed the stock routes.

At dawn, the first rays of the sun lit up the walls in extraordinary hues of red and orange and, buoyed by the spectacle, we were in a

Figure 38: The Buntine Highway, looking back into the Territory from the Western Australia border.

Figure 39: Sawpit Gorge, East Kimberley.

good mood to head into Old Halls Creek, as the mining town is now known.

Old Halls Creek

Old Halls Creek has seen better days. In the 1880s and 1890s, the town was little more than a shanty town of canvas, tin, bark, and spinifex houses. Nevertheless, among the more temporary constructions, there were two hotels, a post office, a gold warden's office, maybe a Police Station and lockup, and I was hoping to see the remnants of these – perhaps renovated in a similar way to those we had seen at Arltunga. It was not to be.

Our first sighting of the old town was of a modern roof and cage constructed over the ruin of the post office and telegraph station. The roof is necessary to protect the mud-brick walls from dissolving into the earth, as it had for decades. The structure stands right next to the road and looks to me as though it was erected just in time. The walls are shadows of their former selves, but if it had not been for the graces of a number of donors and volunteer labourers, we would not have anything left of it at all.

Old Halls Creek was eventually a surveyed and planned community, with neat rows of housing blocks, shops, stores and even a hospital – another Inland Mission Hospital like that at VRD. When we were there, tall grass hid anything left on the ground, but the road signs still identified our location. There is also a concrete memorial to the pioneers, and while we were there, it was having the long grass that surrounded it cut down, before someone put a match to it, I guessed.

In the fields, there are several signs painted on old car bonnets that show the location of the butcher shop and hospital, and there is a row of rock cairns that once held brass information plaques. Clearly, money was once spent on the site in the interest of tourists, but poor maintenance, and the theft of the information plaques and artifacts have left their mark. Sadly, most of them appear to have been

Figure 40: The Halls Creek Post Office and Telegraph Station, protected from the weather.

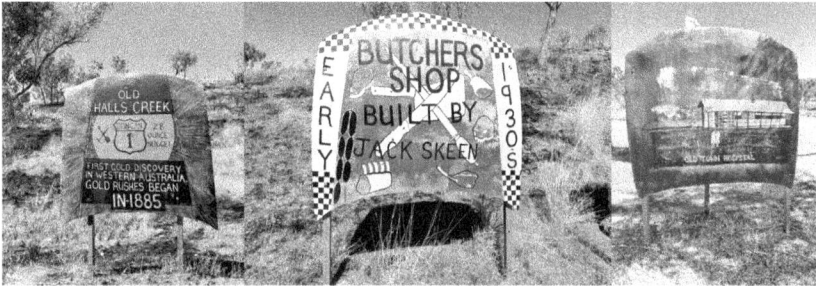

Figure 41: Painted car bonnets identify the locations of several places in Old Halls Creek.

souvenired long ago. If Old Halls Creek was once a ghost town, even the ghosts are now long gone.

Up on the hill, above the post office, there is a lodge and caravan park. The premises are surrounded by junk: old mining equipment, the hulks of trucks and graders, old car bodies and bits and pieces of unidentifiable metal rest undisturbed and secure in their rust.

There were three caravans clustered together in the park, but this early in the season, all the other sites were vacant. I wandered

Figure 42: The Durack Street sign, Old Halls Creek.

over to talk with the owners, and found that they were all one family, here on a gold prospecting expedition from Queensland. They had modern metal detectors and were clearly well prepared for fossicking. The patriarch of the group, Chris, complained that the spinifex and long grass in the bush this year, after the huge wet season, was making it very difficult to prospect. I asked his wife if they had found any gold. She was very circumspect.

"Err, just little bits, here and there," she said.

Clearly, there was no way she was going to share details like that with me. This was the family's third venture to Old Halls Creek, and they were staying several months, so I suspect that they were finding enough gold to pay their way, at least. Chris said the number of prospectors was down this year – the price of fuel for the drive across Australia was crippling the industry, he thought.

No one knows how much gold was taken from around here in the 1880s. A lot of it went out of the Kimberley in people's pockets, including into the Northern Territory, and was never accounted for. The nuggets that Lindsay Crawford and others accepted for the payment of meat, for example, never went through the Gold Warden's books. There is a rumour[42] that a gold buyer regularly took 3,000 ounces of gold out of Halls Creek and it is estimated that as much as 23,000 ounces (nearly 650 kg) of gold was found during the rush – possibly much more.

Unfortunately, the rush only lasted a few months, and men like the Ragged Thirteen were too late to really benefit from it.

Distance was a problem that beset the miners. Once the easy

pickings were taken, it was too expensive to transport machinery, and there was not enough gold found to cover the costs. Many miners left in 1887, especially when other rushes drew their attention. When the Coolgardie rush started, for example, most prospectors were happy to abandon their mines and move on. Some returned during the depression when there was no money or work to be had anywhere else, and they were desperate enough to try their luck here once more.

The longest lasting gold mine of the era struggled on for over 60 years. Known as The Ruby Queen Mine, it closed in 1954, but prospectors like Chris still poke around in the creek beds near it.

Not everyone made it out alive, of course. There are, no doubt, many unmarked graves spread throughout the hills, but the Old Halls Creek Cemetery, just behind the lodge, was easy to find, and sixty-five of the area's pioneers lie here, including the cattleman, Bob Button.

The most obvious grave is particularly noteworthy. It is headed by a large laser-cut depiction of its occupant and the Reverend John Flynn. The occupant is stockman, James (Jimmy) Darcy, who was caught in a cattle stampede in 1917. Darcy was crushed by his horse when it fell in the panic. He suffered massive internal injuries, so his mates took him to the nearest town, Halls Creek, via an agonising 80-mile drive by horse and cart, over a rough stony track.

Unfortunately, the nearest doctor was in Perth, nearly 3,000 km away. The best they could do was to call one, using the telegraph. The local postmaster, Fred Tucket was willing to assist. All he owned to help though, was a sharp, silver, penknife and some good kitchen equipment. Poor Jimmy's bladder had ruptured, and he was on his death bed, but Tucket followed instructions sent by Dr Joe Holland, in Morse code from Perth, and operated on the stricken stockman. Incredibly, the surgery was a success, but Jimmy still needed urgent medical care, so the doctor boarded a cattle ship and headed to Derby. It took a week, then a second week passed, with Holland being driven along half-made roads, across the whole Kimberley region, in a Model T Ford.

Figure 43: The Old Halls Creek Cemetery.

Unfortunately, the car broke down 40 km short of his destination. Undeterred, Holland walked to the nearest cattle station, and borrowed a horse. He then rode through the night and arrived at Halls Creek just as the dawn was breaking – only to hear than Jimmy Darcy had died, several hours earlier, of pneumonia.

His death, however, was not in vain, because Reverend John Flynn, the founder of the Australian Inland Mission in 1912, was moved by the story. Flynn had established the AIM Hospitals we had seen at VRD and Halls Creek, and others in Maranboy, Alice Springs, and Oodnadatta. They were the result of this visionary reverend's horror at the lack of medical care for white people in the bush. Darcy's death in 1917 started Flynn's push for the country's first aeromedical service, designed to give every bushman a 'mantle of safety' and a decade later, the first 'Flying Doctor' set off on his maiden flight, from Cloncurry in Queensland. The Royal Flying Doctor Service was born.

There are sixty-five other graves in the yard, although few have

Figure 44: James Darcy's grave in the Old Halls Creek Cemetery.

headstones. One which does survive is that of thirty-four-year-old Sergeant W. J. Keen, of the West Australian Police. He was buried in May 1889. This was a year before the death of another, Sarah Harriet Berand, who was thirty-seven and, we are told, "a good woman". According to the *Western Mail*[43], Mrs Berand was on the goldfields with her husband and 13 year old daughter. She was one of the very few white women in the area at the time. The reason for her death was not supplied on the headstone.

Sarah was not the first white woman to arrive on the goldfields, at least according to Augustus Lucanus. In his serialised memoirs, published forty years later, he recalled a woman arriving on a camel:

> We soon overtook the camels and three Afghans, and a white woman perched on top of a camel. She was called 'The Maid of the Mountains,' and was the first white woman to come to the goldfields. She came all the way from Queensland. She afterwards went to Wyndham. She was a terrible drunk and spent half her time in the lock up[44].

Another was a woman named 'Mother Dead Finish':

> On the way down [to Hall's Creek} I met a woman driving a five-horse dray like a professional teamster. It was loaded with flour, sugar, tea, etc., also plenty of whisky and rum, and a large crate of fowls. The woman settled for a while at the Denham River. Later she left there for Hall's Creek. I never knew her right name...

These two are remembered as wild drinkers, so it is refreshing to read that Sarah Berand was a 'good woman'.

There is another, much smaller graveyard, containing several tiny graves, across the dirt track from the cemetery gates. The remains of *Ompers*, 'me best mate' *Mug*, and several others, lie there in peace. Mug's grave was particularly flash. He was a much-loved blue heeler, who died at the ripe old age of fifteen.

Old Halls Creek was as far as the Thirteen went as a gang. Merging into the crowd of several thousand hopeful diggers seeking their fortunes at the end of 1886, or in early 1887, the gang split up into pairs or threes, and were no longer a gang, or a threat.

Figure 45: Sarah Berand, a 'good woman' and one of the few women in Halls Creek during the goldrush.

The modern town of Halls Creek was built some fifteen kilometres from the Old Halls Creek in 1955, long after the Thirteen were dead and buried, so it is not a part of their story. The town was built in less rugged terrain closer to the airport, and where there would be room to expand.

Halls Creek is now a thriving centre for local cattle stations and is home to a large Indigenous population, mainly Djaru and Gija people. It is where we headed next.

Halls Creek

My quest was complete at Old Halls Creek, but I needed to visit the new town for fuel for the car and fresh vegetables for the pot. I bought the latter from two Argentinean backpackers at the supermarket. They spoke very little English and had only been in town for two days, so they were not the right people to speak about Halls Creek's history.

I had read stories of a famous miner from the goldrush days who is venerated by this town. He was not a part of the Ragged Thirteen story but, nevertheless, I wanted to see the statue that commemorates him, and find out more. His name was Ivan Fredericks (1864–1904), but he was better known as Russian Jack.

In the late 1880s, Russian Jack was working at the Halls Creek goldmines, like thousands of others. His claim to fame came not from his discovery of gold, but through his strength and loyalty to a friend. When his partner in his mine fell sick, Russian Jack took him 240 km to Wyndham, the nearest town with a medical centre. The remarkable

Figure 46: Russian Jack pushing his sick friend in the wheelbarrow next to the Halls Creek Visitors Information Centre — forever remembered.

part of the story was that he pushed him all the way in a wheelbarrow. It was an immense feat of strength and a powerful demonstration of loyalty to a mate.

The woman working at the Halls Creek Visitors Centre was a proud Gija woman, well aware of the tragic history between her people and the white newcomers 150 years ago. She was also proud of her modern-day hometown and knew its history well. She told me the statue of Russian Jack was erected in 1979, to remember the man, at a cost of about $20,000.

"It's a highlight of the town", she said.

Well good on him, I thought, as we climbed back into the car and started the drive back to Darwin – he deserved commemoration.

I was not surprised that the town has done nothing to commemorate a ragged bunch of bushrangers from the same era. Not one person I met there had heard of them.

Endnotes

1 'Mail-order' was used in the north, even in earliest days of settlement. For example, Fort Victoria's Commandant, John MacArthur, bought his uniforms and boots from Goulburn in N.S.W. and had them sent to Port Essington in the 1830s (see Pugh 2020).

2 *The Canberra Times*, 4 March 1966, Page 11: *Vandal poisons tree.*

3 *Australian Star* (Sydney), 29 October 1907, page 5.

4 The Kilians arrived very early in the Territory's settlement history, in 1873. Mrs Kilian was the Territory's oldest (non-Indigenous) resident when she died in Darwin in November 1926 at the age of 77.

5 *Northern Territory Times and Gazette*, 25 January 1897, page 2.

6 *Sydney Morning Herald*, 19 February 1921, page 14.

7 Banka Banka Station has changed hands several times, and in 2010 the property was purchased by the Indigenous Land and Sea Corporation (ILSC) and managed by the Australian Indigenous Agribusiness company and known as Banka Banka West Station. In 2020, a number of Aboriginal groups were recognised as holding Native Title.

8 Murif, 1897.

9 Walter Baldwin Spencer's Diary, *Spencer and Gillen Expedition, 1901-1902.*

10 White, 1909.

11 Stuart, 1862. Stuart's attack by wild men is at odds with an account collected by Spencer and Gillan, 40 years later, from one of the attackers: The old man had 'actually taken part in the attack on Stuart's party, and from what he told us, we came to the conclusion that Stuart rather exaggerated the capacity of the natives to hinder his progress northwards'. The altercation seems to have been over dwindling water supplies (Spencer & Gillen, 1912).

12 Dropsy is a swelling of the skin because of a build-up of fluid in the body's tissue, these days it is called oedema.

13 See Holmes 1980.

14 *Register*, 8 July 1921, page 8.

15 S.A. Monumental Works, proprietor C. Dunn, had their head office beside the West Terrace Cemetery in Adelaide. With a master stone mason and carver Mr Heddie, they built many of the stone monuments of the 1920s and 1930s, including the soldiers' memorials at Mount Barker, Burra, Port Broughton, Mundoora, and the national war memorial on North Terrace.

16 *The Chronicle*, 12 November 1921, page 16.

17 *Adelaide Advertiser*, 5 May 1919, page 6.

18 The springs feature in an 'Australian Western' called *Bitter Springs* that starred Chips Rafferty and a very young Bud Tingwell in 1950. It wasn't actually filmed at the real Bitter Springs, but it was important because it was empathetic to the Aboriginal experience of colonisation. In a voiceover by 'The Trooper' (Michael Pate) the audience is told:"They call the natives that live there Karagany. The spring has been their tribal home for a thousand years. Two perhaps. Since the time we were savages

anyway. A thousand years. One day, a bloke walks into the government office in Adelaide 800 miles away, bangs down eighty quid, they hand him a bit of stamped paper and Karagany haven't got a tribal home anymore [...] I'll tell you this. They know that waterhole is their tribal ground, and no bit of paper is going to convince them otherwise." (https://www.imdb.com/title/tt0042253). "There is something here" wrote a recent reviewer, "that seven decades later still shows insight and empathy to the early struggles, battles, injustices and hopes that moulded Australia."

19 This species, known as the Mataranka palm, is the same as L. rigida found in isolated populations in Central Australia (Palm Valley). Long thought to be a remnant population from a wetter era, biologists now think the species was carried there by Aborigines during the last 15,000 years (see Trudgen 2012).

20 NBA: Goldsbrough Mort and Co: *Sundry papers re Charles B Fisher and the Northern Australia Territory Co.*, 1886-1892, 2/867/7.

21 *Adelaide Observer*, 11 January 1896, "Troublesome Aborigines", A Chapter from *The Life of a North Australian Pioneer*, by C. E. Gore, page 25.

22 *Northern Territory Times and Gazette* (28 June 1895), Mulligan and Ligar, page 3

23 Ligar lived until 1901, when he died of dysentery on Carlton Station (W.A.) aged 63. Mulligan died on the Fitzmaurice River, north of Katherine on 27 April 1900. He managed the pain of his spear wound by self-medicating and injecting the opiate chlorodyne. Before he died, he 'vomited much blood' and said that 'he was tired, sad, and was going away to his own country'. He was buried at Pine Creek (*Northern Territory Times*, 4 May 1900). For biographies of both these men see Lewis 2022.

24 Linklater, 1997.

25 Lewis, 2012.

26 Lewis, 2012.

27 *Northern Territory Times and Gazette*, 10 April 1896, page 3.

28 *Northern Territory Times and Gazette*, 3 April 1896, page 3, *Drowning at the Katherine*.

29 For an understanding of the importance of the Victoria River Depot and its history see Makin 1999, *The Big Run*, chapter 11.

30 Makin, 1999.

31 Stevens, 1891.

32 *Northern Territory Times*, Tuesday 27 September 1927, page 3, Death of W.J. Schultz 'The Darwin police have received information from the manager of the Victoria River Downs Station, that William Julius Schultz of Humbert River Station, was thrown from his horse and died in Victoria River Hospital on 21st instant'.

33 *Northern Standard*, 18 August 1925, page 2, 'Bush Fatalities'.

34 *Graziers' Review*, 16 September 1926.

35 Lewis, 2022.

36 Faine, 2022.

37 For example, Ted Egan (*Gurindji Blues*), Paul Kelly and Kev Carmody (*From Little Things, Big Things Grow*). See also Ward, *A Handful of Sand*, 2016.

38 The murderer was Charlie Flannigan. He shot Croker over a game of cards one night at Auvergne Station. In 1893, Flannigan became the first man legally executed for his crime in the Territory's history (see Christopherson 2023, and Pugh 2023).

39 *Sydney Morning Herald,* 19 February 1921.

40 A curious reference to Bob Button comes from 1888. He was apparently unwell: "At the Palm Springs, 20 miles from Halls Creek, we were met by a messenger from the Warden to ask the Dr. to come at once, as his services were required for the well-known Mr. R. Button, who had been insane for the last two days" (*Northern Territory Times and Gazette,* 14 July 1888, page 3). He obviously recovered and in 1893 he was prospecting around Halls Creek. He died in Halls Creek in 1911, when managing Ruby Plains Station, aged 58 (SLWA). He was buried in the Halls Creek Cemetery.

41 *Northern Standard,* 22 January 1932, page 5.

42 Halls Creek Visitors Centre

43 *Western Mail,* 7 May 1887.

44 *Daily News,* Friday 30 August 1929, page 6.

Appendix I
A Rhyme of the Ragged Thirteen

The *Sunday Times* published this ballad in Perth in 1938, simply titled *Back-to-the-Goldfields Ballad*[1]. 'Hannons' and 'The Golden Mile' refer to Kalgoorlie, of course, and none of the names of this 'Ragged Thirteen' sounds familiar. However, as some of the original Thirteen headed that way after their failure at Halls Creek, I wonder if there's any connections between them… Is 'Larrikin Green' actually 'Larrikin Bill Smith' for example? Or is this just another rabbit-hole for curious historians to run down?

> The cases of fizz are on the ice, the table turkey's trussed,
> (Hang the bother and hang the price when it's vintage versus dust).
> There's crooners to croon and a band to play, speeches and toasts in turn,
> And all will be in the garden gay where a damper we used to burn.
>
> For it's back to Old Hannans once again, back to the Golden Mile,
> Where the metal still lurks in its diorite den and tailing pyramids pile.
> But this is the song of a splendid band who came in the long ago,
> When Bayley and Ford rocked Groperland with the news of the Golden Blow.
>
> This is the rhyme of the Ragged Thirteen, a baker's dozen of braves.
> Who each lies cold in his lone costean, the best of Outback graves.

The Ragged Thirteen who cut the tracks from Cue to Bayley's Find
The Curse of Thirst upon their backs, a dozen duffers behind.

Aussie and Englishman, Irish and Scotch, Welsh, and Squarehead too,
With never a compass, map, or watch, to bring their brogans through.
Never a pocket that held a bob—the last spree cleared them clean,
A dozen dialects in the mob and the leader was Larrikin Green.

There was Larrikin Green and Paddy the Flat and mighty Mick O'Burn,
Whose fists could beat a rat-tat-tat on a dozen cops in turn,
Wild-Horse Woods and Charlie-the-Goose, Slippery-Dick and Coyle,
Who for forty annuals had a use for a bed above the soil.

Pigweed-Harry and Dry-Soak Sam, Combo Kelly and Sport,
And Scotty, who shot the station ram when the mutton bag ran short.
The thirteenth was a nondescript, long and lousy and lean,
But the gamest man to a singlet stripped was leader Larrikin Green!

It was Green who saved the Warden's life when the Afghan ran amuck;
When the fight was a razor-bladed knife versus Larrikin's pluck.
Green it was who went below when the dynamite was bad
And sent to the brace dead Dan McCrow and Alec Lander's lad.

There may have been a few mishaps when alluvial times were hard,
A few sheep went a-missing, p'r'aps, from Sullivan's slaughter yard.
But when the camp was stiff and cold, and the hospital hadn't a bean
The first to chuck in an ounce of gold was always Larrikin Green.

So, they're holding a Celebration now and fluency's torch will flame,
But none who'll sit at the great pow-wow may recollect his name.
But somehow out in the silent scrub, long leagues from you and me,
Afar from the big palatial pub their bones may restless be.

So, here's to the dog-and-damper days, the days of the dungarees,

When still there was many a track to blaze through slender salmon trees,

When the gay dress suit and motor car were not upon the scene

And the men who steered by a sturdy star were such as Larrikin Green!

Appendix 2
A Ragged Thirteen ghost story

The Ragged Thirteen even made it into the murky world of the occult. Ghost stories were happily told around campfires along the Ord River – and still are. This one was published by the *Western Mail* in 1953[2], and reproduced here because, well, who doesn't like a good ghost story?

> Jim's hair stood on end and his hands came out in a sweat.
>
> Brolga Jim squatted in the flickering circle of the firelight, and the weirdness of his tale seemed to merge with the weirdness of the bush around us. The only sound was the occasional lowing of a bullock from the mob in the shadowy dark behind us, and above the stars blazed like corroboree fires in the Velvet of the Northern Australian night.
>
> It's a strange country, ours, where the unusual is the usual, and the heads and minds of black men and white are still bound closely to the ancient earth which lives and breathes under the spells of the Rainbow Snake and the Sacred Kangaroo.
>
> If you live in the country round the channels of the Ord - through the rest of Australia's cattle country they call it the Underworld - then the river lays her spell upon you, and like the elephant whose days are numbered, you return there to die; that is, if you can break the spell for long enough to leave at all. And more real than the Leprechauns of the Irish bogs and the kelpies of the Scottish moors are the spirits which roam the channels of the Ord. The blackfella spirits of the

animals and birds which belong by rights to other ages; the kaditchas which a man cannot see but which strike death without rhyme or reason; and of course, the spirits of the 'old-timers'; the pioneers who broke the country and jealously watch over its welfare.

"Maluka" was a ragged old ghost who belonged to this last class, and we'd all heard the story of how Maluka roamed the Underworld, striking terror into the hearts of poor drover-men leaving the pubs late at night. He carried an old swag and a blackened billy-can and he tramped the tracks of the Underworld from the mangrove marshes where the river spilled into the sea, right to the red desert of rock a thousand miles to the south. The blacks called him Maluka, which means 'old man', but many a white man claims to have seen him, too. For the past fifty years Maluka's ghost has been a byword in the Underworld, and perhaps we developed a certain proprietary pride in him.

But last night Brolga Jim saw him again. And more than that, he yarned with him. We were squatting round the campfire yarning, as ringers will, when we heard Jim's horse on the track coming back from the town to the camp. Blue Dawg, the heeler, crept in ahead of him towards the fire, his eyes big and brown in the firelight, but the fur along his neck still prickled up in fright.

Jim unsaddled his horse and let him go and then pulled his tobacco pouch from his pocket as he came to the fire. We didn't laugh when he told us he had seen Maluka. The night was too close around us, and beyond the firelight other ghosts were possibly lurking.

Jim told us how he was half asleep in the saddle when Maluka appeared on the track in front of him. His horse snorted with fright and stopped dead, and with a piercing howl Blue Dawg disappeared into the scrub. The spectre lowered the swag he'd been carrying for half a century and said:

"Please, mate, hear me out! I've got a story to tell before I can rest. I've got to clear myself of a crime I never did. Please, mate, hear what an old bushman has to say!"

There was such a note of pleading in the old voice that Jim's heart was touched despite his fright, but anyway he didn't have any option but to hear him because his horse was paralysed on the spot. So, although Jim's hair stood on end and his hands came out in a sweat, he climbed down and squatted there beside old Maluka and patiently heard him out, wondering, because he was a bushman and superstitious at that, whether he'd ever get out of the situation alive.

Fifty years back Maluka and his brother had been prospecting on the rich Halls Creek diggings, washing alluvial gold from the creek. And one happy day they struck a "leader" and panned enough gold in a few days to make them comfortable for the rest pf their lives. In those days, the diggings were like that – plenty of gold about and with a little luck a man was made, but because they were like that there were bad men about, and everyone knew of the reputation of the Ragged Thirteen, a band of robbers on the lookout for easy money. So, Maluka and his brother said nothing of their find, and planned to take the gold to the bank at Darwin for safe keeping, five hundred miles through the scrub, with only station homesteads on the way.

A dozen little calico bags there were, and they sewed them into the lining of their pack saddles and agreed to pretend that they'd fallen out, so that Maluka could load up his belongings and leave the diggings muttering hard words against his brother. That way no one would suspect the find, and when he turned up again in a few weeks it wouldn't matter either. Things often happened that way in the Underworld, land of easy feuds and easier re-unions. It seemed a pretty watertight plan to Maluka, and so it would have been, too, but for the coincidence of another find at the same time.

Unknown to the brothers, three men had made a strike half a mile down the creek, and they, too, kept their secret closely. But closely guarded or not, somehow it leaked out, and the very night that Maluka left the diggings, the Ragged Thirteen raided the camp of the three men and stole their gold in a rough-and-tumble fight. And the men. hearing Maluka had left so suddenly, were quick to violent anger and immediately connected him with the gang and saddled up savagely to track him down.

They caught up with him early in the afternoon, and it was

one against three and Maluka didn't have a chance. They said he was the leader of the Ragged Thirteen, and they knew he had their gold. They pulled down his swag and threw it on the ground and abused him and swore vengeance on him for the sins of the Thirteen. Then a knife bit into the packsaddle lining and one of the bags spilled out. It was a hard land in those days and men often took the law into their own hands. Even while he tried to protest and explain one of them shot him. Then they took his gold and his horses and left him there, his red blood seeping into the groundsheet of his swag. Involuntarily Brolga Jim glanced at the old ghost's swag. The ugly stain was still there.

Well, he didn't die until sundown. He lay there in the hot sun all that afternoon, without his gold and without his good name and he vowed before he died that he'd never take his rest as other dead men did until he'd cleared himself.

But fate plays funny tricks in the land where the heat haze dances at dawn. Before the three prospectors got back to town the real outlaws met up with them. One of the Thirteen had heard the accusation against poor Maluka, and perhaps they had guessed the reason for his sudden departure. There was a gunfight, of course, the three were desperate, for they'd killed a man for their yellow gold, and they still thought he was the leader of this band. They were game, but three were no match for thirteen, and soon the band left them for dead, after having searched them and found the other little bags of gold specks too. But one of them was not dead, and he managed to drag himself to town with the story. He staggered into the bar and told what had happened and roused the miners to a fury. Stealing was one thing, and maybe they'd most of them done a bit of that at one time or another, but murder was a different thing, and they set off in pursuit of the Ragged Thirteen, determined to finish the spate of robberies once and for all. One was dead, they said (that was Maluka) and they would get the others too. They made the pace so hot that the gang were lucky to escape with their lives. But escape they did. They had to split up, but first they planted the gold from the two robberies and agreed to come back for it later, when the hunt had died down.

And the angry miners, riding back to town, saw the black

cloud of hawks circling over Maluka's body, and one of them laughed and another spat, and Maluka's ghost winced and left the body, and set out on the weary quest to find someone who would listen to his tale and clear his name.

Doomed like the Flying Dutchman to wander, the ghost still came back at intervals to the cache of stolen gold, and in the years that followed vengeance came to him in many little ways. As each of the Ragged Thirteen came in turn for the gold, the ghost materialised and taunted them. And he had the perfect right to do so, too, for was not the gold mostly his own? So, one of them fell and broke his leg and died there, and another spilled his canteen of water in his fright and perished two days later of thirst and delirium. Then two of them came together, but when they built their campfire at night, there was Maluka sitting on his swag beside them. Unnerved they began to quarrel, and finally they fought, and one killed the other, and when he saw what he had done he killed himself.

So, after that the Ragged Thirteen were wary, and the little calico bags still lay mouldering where they had been hidden, so legend said. No-one seemed particularly keen to hunt for the gold with so much blood on it, either.

"I'll tell you where it is, for your kindness in hearing me, Brolga Jim!" said the ghost to the drover. But oh no, Brolga Jim was, as I have said, a superstitious man, and he wanted nothing to do with the unlucky gold. There was money for him in the four-footed beasts of the Underworld; its gold was for other folk. Hurriedly he assured Maluka that he would clear his name, so that the poor old ghost could lay down his swag for the last time and pull off his elastic sided boots for ever, but the gold he did not want, for had it not brought bad luck to its rightful owners and everyone else who had had anything to do with it.

Maluka nodded and smiled, and he thanked Jim in a courtly manner for hearing him out. After fifty years, he said, it was great to have a yarn with someone, and he wished he had a bottle of rum to offer Jim a drink for his kindness. Well, Brolga Jim did have a bottle of rum himself in his saddle bag, but he was too scared to mention it, and besides one never quite knew what might happen to a man who drank spirits with spirits, it was bad enough as it was, just talking with one.

But even while he was thinking this, Maluka and his swag faded. The moonlight shone down on the track, and Jim saw the sheen of the lily lagoon through the trees and heard the soughing of a breeze in the boughs.

He knew he hadn't imagined Maluka's visit, for his horse still nickered a little with fright, and then out of the scrub crept Blue Dawg, sorry and sad because he'd deserted his master and still trembling about it, too. Brolga Jim knew that Blue Dawg and the horse could not have imagined the ghost, and moreover, did he not have the whole story now and a promise on him to clear the old ghost's name of the crime which people had mostly forgotten about?

So, he came straight back to the camp and told us about it. When he'd finished talking, nobody said much. I felt glad in a way for old Maluka's ghost, but vaguely disappointed that another legend of the north had ended. It was like the passing of an identity. And though I am a stockman from necessity, I would be a storyteller from choice, and no storyteller hears of the passing of an identity without some small feeling of regret.

But there's still a little more to this story. When we rolled out of our swags this morning and groped for our boots in the half-light, there was a feeling of something different about the atmosphere of the camp; As soon as I got my eyes open properly, I realised that I couldn't see the glow of the fire or hear the clatter of the canteens and the bedourie oven as the cook got breakfast going. Though he was nearly eighty, the Black Snake was a pretty good cook, and regular, too, and it wasn't like him to lag back in his swag after the first flush of piccaninny daylight had streaked the flat-topped hills with rose.

We all looked towards the place he usually slept at once, and there wasn't any swag there, or any sign of the Black Snake either. A couple of pack saddles were gone too, and the half-used bag of flour, and one of the canteens. Then Brolga Jim picked up a ragged scrap of paper anchored down by a pannikin on the waggonette. We saw him squint at it in the half light and then shrug his shoulders. Then, perhaps because I was nearest to him, he handed it to it me to read. The rough-pencilled letters said.

"YOU CAN FORGIT MY CHECK JIM, I WONT NEED IT. I'M THE LAST ALIVE AND NOW THE GHOST WONT GIT ME. I'M GORN BACK TO GIT THAT GOLD."

I looked up and caught Brolga Jim's eye and he shrugged again. Then, because we didn't have a cook to do it, he set about lighting the breakfast fire himself.

Appendix 3

Barney Lamond

In 1920, Barney Lamond wrote down his version of the Ragged Thirteen story for the *Sunday Times* under the heading *Tales of the Early Kimberleys*. His memories of the events of 34 years before are lively and provide an explanation for why the Ragged Thirteen were refused the beef at Abraham's Billabong.

> In the early days of the Kimberley rush, the overland road from Queensland, through the Northern Territory to northern W.A. was the scene of some great adventures, out of which some marvellous yarns were manufactured. Cattle and horse stealing, nigger shooting, wonderful escapes from alligators, snakes and other savage animals, chain lightning rum, De Rougemont, Carr Boyd, all helped.
>
> I myself have struck a few toughies. I won't mention surnames, but they won't mind their nicknames, and though some of them are still kicking round, most have crossed over. There were Boney Brim, Mt. Brown; The Orphan, Green-hide Jack, Billy O'D., Captain Tom of the Ragged Thirteen, Sandy Myrtle, No. 12 in the Ragged Thirteen, or off-sider. I got named Barney M'Coy through singing a song called "Nora, Darling," the chorus of which says she lived happily with her Barney M'Coy, so that a nickname is easily got.
>
> Lots of yarns are told of the Ragged Thirteen, and I think the best of all was when they got the name. It happened at Bitter Springs, on the head of the Roper River, N.T. There is a soak or well there which used to be a great camping place on the road out west. There was a shanty store butchering business [Abraham's Billabong] kept by an old chap, and a rough chap

he was, too, a fighting man with plenty of language and bluff about, but he struck a snag when the Ragged Thirteen came along.

They camped under a big gum tree about 200 yards below the shanty, hobbled out their horses (about 50) and went up to the shanty for a drink – rum, of course. As a matter of fact, there was nothing else in the back country in the outback bungs [the pub owners] kept the casks full and the strength up would make a "Pussyfoot" yell with horror. A pound or two of Barret's twist tobacco fortified it and didn't hurt the colour. A few of those red-backed spiders also, I have heard, were used at times to give it bite; but the daddy of all was 2oz. of vitriol [sulfuric acid]. One chap after a drink sneezed and singed his moustache.

Anyway, to get back to the Ragged Thirteen. They had several juices, and yarned to the other travellers, 30 or 40 of whom were camped there waiting for beef. The shanty keeper had got a beast sent in from the Elsie's Station, 30 miles away, that morning, and it was just killed and hanging on the gallows at the back of the shanty. I might say at that time the cattle in those part suffered from red water disease, which affects fat cattle (it does not affect poor ones), and as soon as you drive them they often drop dead, so that it is hard work to get beef, except by going 30 miles to the station, and they had not had any for three weeks, and practically every pound was sold to the crowd that were waiting and were beef hungry.

The Ragged Thirteen had not had any beef for a long while, and their mouths were watering. When they saw the beef on the gallows they asked the bung (Peter Kerby was his name) if he could let them have 100lb. He said no, it was all sold except some he was keeping for the shanty, and as it had been so hard to get, he wouldn't let them have any of that. They drank more snake juice and got nasty. Peter raged, and told them to and, said he would sooner give it to go to hell, bounced round generally and said he would sooner give it to the blacks than let them have it.

But the Ragged Thirteen went back to their camp smiling. In the morning, the bullock was hanging on the tree at their camp, they having gone up to the yard in the night quartered it and carried it down.

When Peter turned out in the morning and found the beef gone, they say you could hear his roars at the Katherine telegraph station, 200 miles south of Port Darwin. He awoke most of the chaps camped close to the shanty, and one of them said he saw beast hanging on a gum tree down the creek, "where those fellows were camped that he was rowing with last night."

Peter rushed down, followed by the crowd who had been promised beef, called them thieving skunks, that if they didn't have that beef back on the gallows in five minutes he would bump every mother's son of them. Sandy Myrtle said, "One at a time," and he [illegible] in and gave … real good tanning in two rounds, cut up the beef there and then, divided it among all the travellers, kept 100lb. for themselves, but didn't give Peter the shanty keeper even a shank, nor did they pay a bean for the bullock.

That was the start of the Ragged 13 and how they got their name. They went from there to the Victoria River, Fisher Lyons' station, and what happened then is another yarn[3].

MORE ESCAPADES in the KIMBERLEY RUSH

On leaving the Roper, the crowd who enjoyed the fun and cheap beef presented the Ragged 13 with a demijohn of chain lightning rum and wished them good luck and plenty of gold. They struck across for Delamere, 90 miles from the Victoria River. The first stage was the Dry River, 40 miles, where there was a big clay waterhole. The country here is rich and clayey, and full of cracks, like the Barcoo in Queensland; you could chuck a jam-tin in them out of sight.

When the 13 struck this clay hole it was just thick mud, having been churned up by a mob of Delamere cattle, which had left their tracks going straight on for the river. The Dry River was dry, and so were the 13, it having been a hot day (116 in the waterbag) and their coppers being the same, they had had several gargles and lowered the water level.

There was nothing for it but to camp. They just tossed off the packs, hobbled out the neddies, and dossed down anywhere. Most of them chewed some of the shanty raw beef for moisture, but none of them wanted any chain lightning, and none wanted to smoke. Some slept. It was a red-hot night.

About 3 o'clock in the morning one of those Territory showers came along – 3 inches in about half an hour, with thunder and lightning. No wonder there are no tall trees in that country. The downpour made the camp very boggy, and the horses took a bit of collecting, as green-hide hobbles don't stand bog much, and everything in the camp was wet and miserable, except the rum.

Two days later they struck the Victoria River, about 20 miles below the Fisher Lyons cattle station, one of the biggest herds in that part of the North. They picked a big Leichardt pine, one that throws a quarter of an acre shade for a camp, and decided on a day's spell to wash up, mend hobbles, sleep, fish, smoke, and yarn. About 4 o'clock in the afternoon they saw a chap coming along with a mob of pack horses and two black boys, who turned out to be gins in moles and shirts.

He rode up to the camp, got off to have a pitch, asked where they came from and where they were going to. Had they called at the Roper Shanty? If they had, did they strike the Ragged 13, and which way were they going? They answered that they came from Queensland and were going to the Kimberley goldfield. Yes, they had called at the Roper; the 13 were there and going to Halls Creek.

Just imagine how news travels in the back country-mulga wires, almost as fast as wireless. They had only been five days coming 200 miles; and the news was on the river before them. This chap, who turned out to be the storekeeper Johnny who before he left their camp, said: "Tell the 13 not to come near the station or they will get a hot reception, but no stores for love or money."

Capt. Tom said: "What's the matter with them, anyhow? They only commandeered a bit of beef when they could not buy it."

The storekeeper Johnny asked them to describe the 13. What was the captain like? Tom described himself as a tall, dark, fierce-looking man, 6ft 2in. long, black moustache, with a pointed beard-in fact, he painted them like a lot of Italian brigands. It was rather amusing, as he was a short bloke, with a red face, red beard, and whiskers.

Now, the Fisher Lyons store at the station was known all over the country, where travellers could get good rations, and the 13 intended to buy a supply there. They had a good talk over this matter before they shifted camp next day and went on to camp near the station the following night.

They decided that as the storekeeper would not let them have food at any price, they would take it first and pay after. They expected there would be more mulga wires through saying who they were before they left the river. When they reached the station, they camped below the Norde. The next evening, they went up, had a yarn, and looked round. They found the store was a large building by itself, made of upright logs let into the ground and securely fastened with a chain and padlock. They said, "Good night" and went back to their camp.

Later they returned with packbags, took three or four logs out of the side of the store, filled their bags with what they wanted, replaced the logs, and went back to camp. In the morning, they packed up and rode to the station. All hands came out to see them, and the storekeeper asked them if they wanted any rations. Capt. Tom said. "No, thank you, as we are the Ragged 13, and you said that we should not get any stores for love nor money. We have taken what we want. Here is a list of the goods, and if you make up the bill we will pay for them."

Well, you could have knocked the Johnny down with less than a feather. All the stockmen laughed. But he came to and raged round and ordered one of the chaps to get horses and packs to go into the Katherine – 400 miles – and telegraph to Port Darwin for the police. But none of them would go for him. Capt. Tom advised him not to do that, as in 200 miles they (the 13) would be out of the Territory and over in W.A. He said it would be better to send to Roebourne, 1000 miles, and wire to the police in Perth. He then said, "Good day," and started for the Ord River[4].

Endnotes

1   'Dryblower' *Sunday Times* (Perth), 21 August 1938, page 21.
2   *Western Mail* (Perth), 30 April 1953, page 3.
3   *Sunday Times*, 7 November 1920.
4   *Sunday Times*, 21 November 1920.

Bibliography

Ashwin, A. C. (2002). *Gold to Grass: The reminiscences of Arthur C. Ashwin, 1850-1930 prospector & pastoralist*. Perth: Hesperian Press, Peter Bridge (Ed.).

Barron, G. (2019). *Red Jack and the Ragged Thirteen*. Haymarket: Stories of Oz.

Browne, T. A. (1888). *Robbery Under Arms. Retrieved from Gutenberg*: https://www. gutenberg.org/cache/epub/1198/pg1198-images.html

Browning, C. (2001). *Ordinary Men: Reserve Police Battalion 11 and the Final Solution in Poland*. London: Penquin.

Buchanan, R. (1997). *In the Tracks of Old Bluey*. Brisbane: Queensland University Press.

Bucknall, G. (2008). Robert Bruse Plowman. In D. Carment, A. Powell, R. Maynard, B. James, & H. Wilson, *Northern Territory Dictionary of Biography* (pp. Vol 2, p 472). Darwin: Charles Darwin University Press. Retrieved from Northern Territory Dictionary of Biography.

Christopherson, D. (2023). *A Little Bit of Justice*. Darwin: CDU Press.

Clement, C., & Bridge, P. (1991). *Kimberley Scenes*. Perth: Hesperian Press.

Cook, D. (2010). *The Ragged Thirteen*. Retrieved from Our Outback Family: https://www. campertraileraustralia.com.au/Destination/11689/Our_Outback_Family

Creaghe, E. C. (1883). *The Diary of Emily Caroline Creaghe: Explorer*. Edited with Introduction by Peter Monteath: Corkwood Press, 2004.

Cross, J. (2011). *Great Central State: The Foundation of the Northern Territory*. Adelaide: Wakefield Press.

Drake, J. (2012). *The Outback vs the Wild West*. Brisbane: Boolarong Press.

Durack, M. (1959). *Kings in Grass Castles*. London: 1986 edition, Corgi.

Durack, M. (2023, December 29). *Australian Dictionary of Biography*. Retrieved from William Henry James Carr-Boyd (1852-1925). written in 1969.: https://adb.anu. edu.au/biography

Dutton, D. (2011). *The Psychology of Genocide, Massacres, and Extreme Violence: Why*

"Normal" People Come to Commit Atrocities. London: Bloomsbury 3PL.

Faine, J. (2022). *Apollo and Thelma: A true tall tale.* Melbourne: Hardie Grant Publishing.

Forrest, A. (1880). *North-West Exploration: Journal of Expedition from DeGrey to Port Darwin.* Perth W.A.: see nla.obj-33599498 National Library of Australia.

Gaunt, C. (1931 -1934, A serialised memoir). *Old Time Memories.* Northern Standard.

Green, N. (1995). *The Forrest River Massacres.* Fremantle: Fremantle Arts Centre Press.

Gunn, J. (1907). *We of the Never Never* (15th ed.). New York: McMillan.

Hill, E. (1951). *The Territory.* Sydney: Walkabout Pocketbook edition, 1970.

Holmes, K. (1980). *The White Range Settlement Area. Arltunga Goldfield, Northern Territory: A look at the lifestyle of an isolated mining area.* https://core.ac.uk/download/pdf/41229983.pdf: Accessed 17 April 2024.

James, B. (1995). *Occupation Citizen: The Story of Northern Territory Women and the Vote (1894-1896).* Darwin: James.

Jones, T. (1987). *Pegging the Northern Territory: A history of mining in the Northern Territory, 1870-1946.* Darwin: N.T. Department of Mines and Energy.

Jones, T. (Vol. 2, September 2004). Adam Johns: Prospector, Miner & Explorer of the Northern Territory 1840-1896. *Journal of Australasian Mining History,* https://www.mininghistory.asn.au/wp-content/uploads/10.-Jones.

Lamond, G. A. (1986). *Tales of the Overland: Queensland to the Kimberley in 1885.* Perth: Hesperian Press.

Lewis, D. (2004). *A Wild History: life and death on the Victoria River frontier.* Melbourne: Monash University Press.

Lewis, D. (2022, December 9). *Victoria River District Doomsday Book.* Retrieved from https://doi.org/10.31235/osf.io/kfmnz: https://doi.org/10.31235/osf.io/kfmnz

Linklater, W., & Tapp, L. (1997). *Gather No Moss.* Perth: Hesperian Press. First published 1968 by Macmillan Co.

Lockwood, D. (1964). *Up the Track.* Adelaide: Rigby, Seal Books.

Lumholtze, C. (1889). *Among Cannibals.* https://commons.wikimedia.org/wiki/File:Dispersal.jpg.

Marr, D. (2023). *Killing for Country.* Collingwood: Black Inc.

Millett, P. (no date). *The Duracks of Argyle: A summary of pioneering venture and the years 1852-1950 in Kimberley W.A.* Western Australia: Quality Press.

Murif, J. J. (1897). *From Ocean to Ocean: Across a Continent on a Bicycle: An Account of a Solitary Ride From Adelaide to Port Darwin.* Melbourne: https://www.gutenberg.org/ebooks/58206.

Parsons, J. L. (1886). *Half-Yearly Report on Northern Territory to December 31, 1886*. Adelaide: Library and Archives of the Northern Territory.

Playford, P. (2023, November 30). *The Discovery Of The East Kimberley Goldfield 1885*. Retrieved from Kimberley Society, 2005: https://kimberleysociety.org/oldfiles

Playford, P., & Ruddock, I. (1985). Discovery of the Kimberley Goldfield: Early Days. *Royal Western Australian Historical Society Journal and Proceedings*, Vol 9.

Pugh, D. (2020). *Port Essington: The British in North Australia 1838-49*. Darwin: www.derekpugh.com.au.

Pugh, D. (2021). *Darwin: Growth of a City: The 1880s*. Darwin: www.derekpugh.com.au.

Pugh, D. (2022). *Twenty to the Mile: The Overland Telegraph Line*. Darwin: www.derekpugh.com.au.

Purtill, A. (2014). *Survivors of 'forgotten' Woolwonga tribe acknowledged 130 years after 'extermination'*. Retrieved from National Unity: http://nationalunitygovernment.org

Purvis, A. (1946-8). *Heroes Unsung*. Alice Springs: Unpublished manuscript, see Territory Stories https://hdl.handle.net/10070/431887.

RegisterDeaths. (1870s). Medical Officer, Register of Deaths, District of Palmerston, 1872-1890. Northern Territory Archives.

Reynolds, H. (1989). *Dispossession: Black Australians and White Invaders*. Allen & Unwin, p. 52.

Roberts, T. (2005). *Frontier justice : a history of the Gulf country to 1900*. Brisbane: University of Queensland Press.

Roberts, T. (2009, September 14). *The Brutal Truth: What happened in the Gulf Country*. Retrieved from The Monthly: https://www.themonthly.com.au/issue/2009/november/

Robinson, J. (2002). *The Ragged Thirteen: Stories of Australia's Northern Frontier in the 1880s*. Brisbane: Queensland University Press.

Rose, A. (1964). *Early Northern Territory Droving Epics*. Alice Springs: Australian Veterinary Journal, Vol 40, March 1964.

Searcy, A. (1909). *In Australian Tropics*. London: George Robertson and Co.

Searcy, A. (1912). *By Flood and Field: Adventures Ashore and Afloat in North Australia*. London: G. Bell and Sons, 1st Edition.

Smith, R. (2024). *Licence to Kill: Massacre Men in Australia's North*. Darwin: Historical Society of the Northern Territory.

Sowden, W. (1882). *The Northern Territory as it is: a narrative of the South Australian Parliamentary party's trip and full description of the Northern Territory, its settlements and industries*. Adelaide: W.K. Thomas.

Spencer, B., & Gillen, F. (1912). *Across Australia* (2nd Edition Vol. 2 ed.). London: MacMillan and Co.

Spencer, W. B. (2024, April 17). *Spencer's Diary from the Spencer and Gillen Expedition 1901-1902.* Retrieved from Researchgate: https://www.researchgate.net/publication/320741186_Walter_Baldwin_Spencer's_Diary

Stevens, H. (1887, April 30). Stevens, H.W.H. to Goldsbrough Mort & Co. *letters received from H. W. H. Stevens, Port Darwin, re NT property and butchering.* Goldsbrough Mort & Company Records. NBA, 2/872., In Lewis, 2017.

Stevens, H. (1891, June 1). Victoria River Downs Improvements. *Head Office, Melbourne: letters received from H.W.H. Stevens, Port Darwin, re NT Melbourne: letters received from H.W.H. Stevens, Port Darwin, re NT.* Goldsbrough Mort & Company Records. NBA 2/872. In Lewis 2022.

Stuart, J. M. (1862). *Explorations in Australia: The Journals of John McDouall Stuart During the Years 1858, 1859, 1860, 1861, When he Fixed the Centre of the Continent and Successfully Crossed It from Sea to Sea.* Online: http://www.gutenberg.org/ebooks/8911 accessed December 2020.

Swan, D. (1991). Kimberley Scenes. In C. Clement, & P. Bridge, *Kimberley Scenes* (pp. pp 84-129). Perth: Hesperian Press.

Thompson, G. (2024, January 12). *Thompson's List of Halfcastes in the Northern Territory, 1899.* Retrieved from Northern Territory Archives Service: https://dtc.nt.gov.au/__data/assets/pdf_file/0005/268007/ntrs790_10441_transcirpt.pdf

Traine, T. (2005). *Life and Adventure in Northern Australia.* Perth: edited by Peter J Bridge, Hesperian Press.

Traynor, S. (2016). *Alice Springs: From singing wire to iconic outback town.* Adelaide: Wakefield Press.

Trudgen, M., Webber, B., & Scott, J. (2012). Human-mediated introduction of Livistona palms into central Australia: conservation and management implications. *Proc. R. Soc. B.2794115–4117*, p. https://royalsocietypublishing.org/doi/10.1098/rspb.2012.1545.

Ward, C. (2016). *A Handful of Sand: The Gurindji Struggle After the Walkoff.* Melbourne: Monash University Press.

Webber, E. (December 2022). *The Ragged Thirteen, a Matter of Opinion.* National Trust eNews.

White, G. (1909). *Across Australia.* London: Society for the Promotion of Christian Knowledge.

Willshire, W. (1896). *Land of the Dreaming.* Online, downloaded from: https://www.forgottenbooks.com/.

Index

C

D

Y

Yanyuwa 1

Further readings

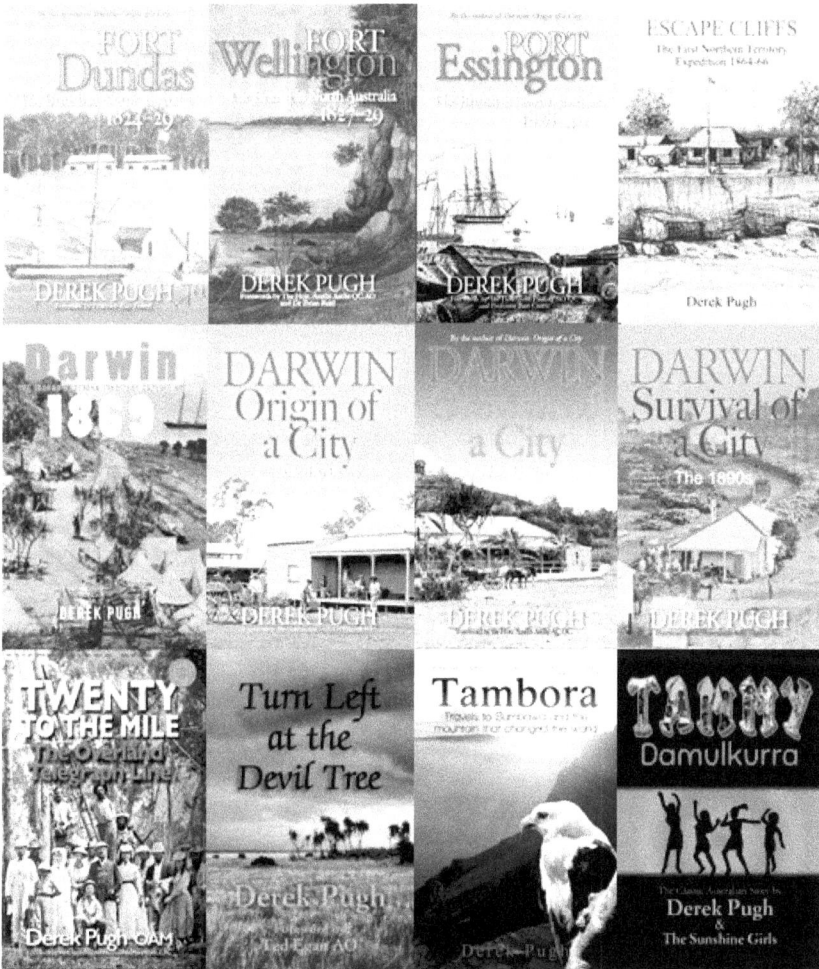

www.derekpugh.com.au

www.ingramcontent.com/pod-product-compliance
Lightning Source LLC
Chambersburg PA
CBHW060022100426
42740CB00010B/1560